OUTSPOKEN!
Essays On Things that Matter

By

Roger W. Hite

Other Titles by Roger Hite

Trumping the Queen (2016)
Poetry Trumps Prose (2016)
Ditch Santa! (2015)
Growing Old: The Best Is Yet to Be (2015)
America, Going to Hell in A Handbasket: A Boomer's
Political Lament (2015)
Presidential Voices of My Time (2015)
A Blessed Duck! (2015)
The Shoe-Box Miracle (2015)
Mission before Margin (2015)
Beautiful Lies (2015)
Re-Wrapping Christmas (2014)
Crappy Medicine (2014)
The Green Sash Mentors (2014)
Separation of Church and State (2014)
But for the Grace of God (2014)
Relishing Two Decades of Spring (2014)
A Stack of Newspapers (2014)
The Inheritance (2013
A Gospel of Organizational Leadership (2013)
My Life's Work (2013)
My Media Nanny (2013)
Still Kicking! (2013)
The Mule-Kicker's Dialogues (2013)
Roger's Run (2012)
Bonnie's Time (2012)
The Great Health Care Decision (2012)
Dog-Mom (2011)
The Nun of Camelot (2011)

From Groundhog Day to Camelot (2010)
I Still Buy Green Bananas (2010)
The Return to Marlboro (2010)
Unwrapping Christmas (2009)
Last Stop before Paradise (2009)
Buster's View (2009)
The Loser (2008)
Buster's Spirit (2008)
The Iron Butterfly (2008)
Nesting Among Ducks (2008)
Cottage by the Sea (2007)
The Foul Game (2007)
Vivid Imagination (2005)
The Sister Deal (2004)
The God Switch (2004)
Soul Merchants (2004)
Buster's View (2002)
Mirror Man (2001)
The Twelve Candle Miracle (1999)
What's the Good Word? (1999)
The Ebony Snowflake (1999)
The Art of Awe (1998)
Our Gift (1998)
Buster at My Side (1997)
Buster at the Gate (1995)
Buster at the Wall (1994)

DEDICATION

"To Dr. Lou Osternig—a dear friend, former undergraduate track-team member, and a fellow Oregon Duck I have known for half-a-century! Someone who tolerates an outspoken Republican!"

PREFACE

I am one of those persons who loves to think about things that matter and then do my best to express my thoughts and feelings on the printed page.

There is something exciting and satisfying about seeing my thoughts dance across the screen of my computer as I try and make sense out of things that matter to me.

Since retiring and moving to Eugene Oregon in 2008, I have enjoyed writing essays on a wide variety of topics. It might be a correct term to say I am "Outspoken" when it comes to expressing my feelings about political and social subjects that are in the news and being discussed nationally and locally.

Many of these essays were submitted for publication in the Register-Guard newspaper here in Eugene. Some were published, some were discarded by the editors for reasons I never worried about and didn't take personally.

In the following pages I express my views on a wide variety of topic ranging from presidential politics, health care policies, minimum wage controversy, paying college athletes, and a host of other topics. The essays were written over a five-year period. The first two essays are personal in nature and were added while watching the 2016 Olympics in Rio.

There is no rhyme or reason to the sequence of essays contained in this collection. I simply wanted to preserve them by removing them from the digital archive of my computer and file them in a single place for future reference.

Why? Because I can.

Dr. Roger Hite, August, 2016

1

"The Olympics Trumps Presidential Politics"

It was a great national blessing. The Olympics arrived just in time to "trump" presidential politics! Amen! Praise the Lord! There is a Supreme Being who delivers us from the evils of demagogic rhetoric!

A beleaguered American public was able to take a much needed deep-breath as it settled into two-weeks of Olympic competition. There was an unintended consequence of being a couch-potato for an endless stream of commercials interspersed by awesome athletic competition. The Olympics relieved Americans of the painful rhetorical sparring between political competitors Donald Trump and Hillary Clinton.

The popularity of the Olympics also exposed a great truth about how public perceptions are managed by the mainstream media. The media selects what it thinks is important to its liberal political agenda and converts it into sound-bite reality that it hopes will shape the American political culture. Sometimes, however, the "virtual reality" created by the media is eclipsed by the true reality of important events—not contrived importance like campaign rhetoric. The Olympics will always come in first when it comes to what is valued the most by the American public. Why? Because it isn't driven by people in quest of money and power—like many politicians. It is driven by the pure desire for competitors to show they are the best in their events—not the person who talks the greatest game—but the person who displays they are indeed the best. The Olympics are about actions and not words—about achievements and not promises.

The presidential race, by contrast, isn't about demonstrating anything but rhetoric—it is about personalities and political promises and not tested policies.

By contrast, the coverage of the Olympics exposes which competitor best fulfills their promises they are indeed the superior competitor.

The big story is no longer what either presidential candidate says while on the campaign hustings. The big story is Usain Bolt winning the gold medal in the 100 meters over his rival American sprinter Justin Gatlin. The big story is how the women's gymnastics team won the gold medal. Or, how the greatest Olympic swimmer of all-times, American Michael Phelps ended his competitive career by winning his 23 Olympic Gold Medal.

On the back-stage of America presidential politics the rhetoric of demagoguery continued to be spewed by both Donald Trump and Hillary Clinton.

Unlike the Olympics when the preliminary races produce the highest quality performers in their respective Olympic events, this year's presidential qualifying heats produced two very mediocre competitors.

How fitting it was that the prelude to the final months of the Presidential campaign was sidetracked by the Olympics. If nothing else, it provided a reminder that in athletics, unlike American politics, there is a process that brings the best competitors into the final events.

Sadly, neither Trump nor Clinton represent the finest and best competitors in this year's presidential race. Trump continues to stumble out of the blocks and Hillary does her best to use the performance enhancing drugs of the Democratic establishment's political machinery to maintain a steady lead over the faltering Donald Trump.

Donald Trump's rhetoric seems to continue to fall back on the charge that the American political system is "rigged" and doesn't give a fair chance to all competitors. Hillary Clinton's rhetoric focuses on the notion that she does not face a "worthy" competitor, but someone who is not qualified to stand at the top of the award podium and have the gold metal placed around his neck.

In politics, the silver medal of runner-up is not held in high esteem—indeed, it is the symbol of "the first loser."

Unlike the Olympics when the campaign produces its "winner" and everybody goes home to bask in *the thrill of Victory and the agony of Defeat,"* there are continuing serious consequences to the outcome of the campaign competition. The victor's work has just begun when the shouting of the victory lap subsidizes. The President has the burdensome task of actually leading one of the most complex organizations in the world.

Winning the campaign doesn't simply put a trophy and a medal in a competitor's personal showcase. As much as the media loves to create drama and build up to the election night "race," once the contest is won, then the competitor has to hang up the competitive spikes and don the "sweat suit" of leadership.

The great tragedy of this Presidential race is that once the "gold medal" is awarded, the public and the media must come to terms with the reality that our political system is indeed "rigged" so that money continues to corrupt all the politicians who "won their election contests" and move into the halls of congress.

To stretch the metaphor, money is the "performance enhancing drug"—the PED—that is ruining our political system. The tragedy is that the Money PED is indeed addictive. Once one is elected our system immediately addicts the winners to continue with the drug. Indeed, their political parties instruct the winners that their new "training" regime involves spending upwards of thirty-hours a week actively soliciting funds for their respective parties.

The real challenge for whoever wins the "Gold" and stands atop the political award stand in November is to clean up the system and start the long process of rehabilitating a political system that is addicted to money.

Is either candidate really up to this daunting task?

2

"A Leap of Faith"

Watching world-class long-jumpers compete in the Olympic long jump event brought to my mind an important philosophical metaphor—a "leap of faith."

Every human has at some time during their journey down life's runway attempted to make "a leap of faith." Some succeed, some fail, but the challenge awaits everyone who has ever lived.

What is a "leap of faith?" It is what we do when we finally come to terms with what we believe as contrasted with what we know. Faith is what suspends us in life between the "toe board" of knowledge from which we leap and the unknown spot in the "sands" of beliefs.

The choice is binary for all who compete in life. You either make the leap or you don't. Unlike in the Olympics, your victory is not in how far you leap, but that you have the courage to attempt the leap. The leap of faith is its own reward.

Anyone who is a Christian has successfully made the leap of faith. What kind of training makes the leap successful?

To begin with, one has to acknowledge that the story of creation and the beginning of the world is in fact "a story." It is, however, a story inspired by God and written by men.

For Christians who use the Bible as their "training manual" for their leap of faith, the early story of how it all began is contained in Genesis. It was written by humans with limited scientific knowledge of the world and the cosmos as we know it today. The writers thought the Earth was flat and that it was the center of our universe. The early religious scriptures were God's way of giving humans a starting point to understand what was impossible to know given the sparse scientific knowledge of the early Biblical times.

Such a story helped humanity to understand something beyond their comprehension. It wasn't a lie or a deception, but a starting point for "believing" that an all-powerful Creator was the genesis of all creation. The story allowed early civilization to take its own "leap of faith" and formulate a belief about the nature of their world and their God.

Many stories in the Bible are parables, metaphors, and figurative expressions of Truths. Our leap of faith allows us to rise above the need to somehow bring "cognitive balance" and ignore the "cognitive dissonance" one has to overcome in making sense out of everything that is written in the Bible. It took me decades to stop fretting about whether certain things were "literal" of "figurative" as they were written in the pages of the Jewish and Christian scriptures of the Old and New Testaments. I no longer try to make sense out of someone being swallowed by a whale and regurgitated days later. I no longer try to understand the complex symbolism and allegorical messages contained in the book of Revelations.

What, then, is essential to my personal "leap of faith?" What is the core of my faith?

I believe that the earliest Jewish prophets wrote about a future arrival of a "Messiah." That person was conceived by a divine miracle in the womb of the virgin girl Mary. Jesus was "God" in human flesh. He walked the earth and performed miracles. He raised people from the dead and transformed water into wine. He multiplied a few fishes and loaves and fed a mass of several thousand. He fulfilled prophecy and was crucified on the Cross. He rose from the dead three days after his death. Before his final ascension into Heaven he gave his disciples the Holy Spirit—a spirit that is indwelling in all Christian followers and gives them daily connection with Jesus and God the father. Jesus will fulfill his promise to return once again and bring to a conclusion this finite episode of life on earth as we know it. There will be a day of judgment and reconciliation. Ultimately, Good will prevail over Evil. Justice will overcome injustice.

In conclusion, my leap of faith lands me firmly in the sands of human existence. It allows me to believe that Christ's sacrifice on the cross was redemptive for all believers. It was done in atonement for humanity's sinful behavior. Believing in this allows all to transcend mortal life and live in eternity with our Creator.

There are endless things that challenge me daily in my leap of faith. In my airborne state suspended between the hard facts of life and the seeming cognitive dissonance between what I know and what I believe, it is my faith that sustains me.

I have finally come to the conclusion that human logic and reasoning is the practical gift humans have been given by God to run through the race we call life. It is a good gift that serves us well until we try to use it to achieve "cognitive consistency" with everything we encounter in our life's race.

I used to tell the management team at the hospital where I was one of the leaders, "If you don't measure something, you can't manage it." I also cautioned, "If you try to measure everything, you won't manage anything."

These principles also apply to one's "leap of faith." If you don't have a set of a few things around which you launch your "leap of faith," then you cannot be successful in moving from knowledge to belief. Your leap has to be predicated on the reality that you cannot know everything and make sense of everything. Faith requires the willful suspension of disbelief and letting go of the need to understand what is beyond human comprehension.

I don't try to make sense of everything. I act on believing a few things. Central to my leap of faith is a belief that Christ is the son of God, he lived and died to demonstrate to all of humanity that faith is the only enduring thing that allows us to gain peace and optimism in our life's journey.

Unlike the Olympic athletes striving to have the longest leap, in the leap of faith there is no reward for one who shows the greatest performance. The gold medal of daily peace and eternal salvation is given to all who make the leap of faith.

There is nothing to lose in making the leap of faith and everything to gain. Faith makes Olympians out of all of us.

3

"Beware of *Post-Hoc* Political Pronouncements"

In light of Mr. Jonah Goldberg's April 27th Register-Guard editorial *"Clinton Foundation may be Achilles' Heel"* it is time to sharpen our critical thinking and reasoning skills as the 2016 presidential campaign begin gearing up to bombard our senses with political rhetoric. Specifically, it is time to caution readers to be on guard for the fallacy of post hoc reasoning that Mr. Goldberg seems to be leaning toward accepting in the case of Hillary Clinton's role as Secretary of State.

I am not an apologist for former Secretary of State Hillary Clinton or former President Bill Clinton—I know they are far more adept in defending their actions than I am. I am, however, a critical thinker who has difficulty with the current political climate undermining Hillary Clinton's presidential campaign.

I have heard much political chatter about the upcoming book CLINTON CASH—an expose written by Mr. Peter Schweizer—a Hoover Institute Researcher, Oxford scholar, and conservative author who previously published a scathing analysis of how all politicians who enter Congress—whether republicans or democrats—emerge far wealthier than when they take office. I was struck at the balanced information contained in his book THROW THEM ALL OUT and recommended it to friends and former colleagues. It reinforced my preference that all members of Congress focus on governing and making laws, not putting priority on fundraising for their next political campaign.

A motive for timing his new book isn't hard to infer. The publisher is a subsidiary owned by Fox News. It is aimed at attacking Mrs. Clinton's integrity and derailing her presidential campaign. The book alleges Hillary is culpable of using her position to peddle her influence to sources that consequently made large contributions to the family-owned Clinton Foundation.

I watched the recent Fox news program outlining all of the so-called questionable ways in which Hillary Clinton's actions allegedly secured huge speaking fees for her husband. The program inferred how some of her decisions while Secretary of State allegedly led to huge contributions to the Clinton Foundation from sources who benefited from actions taken during her term as Secretary of State.

When the book comes out on May 5th, it will probably become an instant best seller—given the reality that Hillary Clinton is in the political limelight as the front-running democrat for its party's candidate in 2016. Like many, I intend to get a copy and judge for myself if there is any evidence of inappropriate and potentially illegal actions on the part of the Clinton's.

I don't presume to tell people how to read the book or to prejudice how they digest the information it contains. I do want to caution everybody who reads the book and/or listens to political pundits pontificate on the book's contents, to beware of the logical fallacy knows as *Post Hoc Ergo Propter Hoc*—or simply called "**the post hoc fallacy**."

The Latin expression translates literally into "*after this, therefore because of this*." Such a logical fallacy is based on the kind of thinking that assumes "since event Y followed event X, event Y must have been caused by event X. Such fallacious reasoning is tempting because the time sequence appears to be integral to causality. This fallacy lies in coming to a conclusion based "solely" on the order of events, rather than taking into account other factors that might rule out the logical connection. Such a fallacy can easily be seen when we assert that *"a rooster crows before the sunrises, therefore the rooster is the cause of the sunrise."*

The recent FOX News Special television program featured an interview with Mr. Schweizer about the forthcoming book. He gave example after example of how events happened during Hillary Clinton's tenure as Secretary of State that resulted in favorable outcomes for several foreign governments and business organizations. Shortly after such decisions the benefitted made sizeable contributions to the Clinton Foundation—and some gave huge speaking fees to former President Bill Clinton.

In the televised interview the author builds a circumstantial argument case for asserting a causal link between Hillary Clinton's being Secretary of State and the contributions by benefactors for favorable governmental rulings during her tenure in office. To use another Latin expression, he asserts there was a *"Quid pro quo"* cause-to-effect relationship.

Please read the book with a critical eye for whether Mr. Schweizer provides any additional evidence or documents supporting his claim of impropriety in Mrs. Clinton's behavior other than the fact that after favorable rulings benefitting an entity, such an entity made a major contribution to the Clinton Foundation—and that huge speaking fees were paid to her husband and former President Bill Clinton were caused by Mrs. Clinton's behavior.

I am quite certain the information contained in Mr. Schweizer's book will play a major role in shaping the judgments voters make regarding the integrity and the trustworthiness of Mrs. Clinton's candidacy. I am equally certain that this early *"ad hominem"* attack is just the beginning of a brutal presidential campaign by both parties—a campaign that will focus too much on the personalities of candidates rather than on evaluating the appropriateness of the plans they advocate to strengthen America in the years of their presidential administration.

I hope, however, that voters who read CLINTON CASH will not fall prey to the fallacy of post hoc reasoning when they draw their conclusions about Mrs. Clinton's integrity. I hope potential voters look at something more than simply the sequence of events. We should presume the innocence of the Clintons unless there is specific evidence of foul play. Don't let post hoc reasoning short-circuit critical analysis of all the forthcoming political rhetoric from both parties—even professional political journalists like Goldberg appears susceptible.

4

"A Political Incorrect Perspective"

Those of us who are card-carrying conspiracy theorists are reveling in all the scenarios embedded in the political turmoil surrounding this upcoming mid-term congressional election. Be thankful you are not an incumbent and/or not linked to the Obama administration. Maybe that's exactly what Ron Emanuel is thinking!

It may appear on the surface that the so-called Tea Party is the product of some kind of spontaneous combustion or "big bang theory" that has created a new Great Awakening of American evangelical politics. Wrong!

At the national convention of conspiracy theorists held recently—but denied by all of us—members affirmed a long held premise regarding the success of President Obama.

Those who control the world (TWCTW) conspired to put their resources behind the candidacy of the idealistic, articulate, personable black senator from Illinois and help organize the populist groundswell of "change now" rhetoric that got him elected to the most powerful political position in the world.

Sadly, Mr. Obama did not have a clue about the forces behind the American political scene that engineered his election. He simply thought he was the man of the hour and destiny had dealt him the winning hand. That is the way it is supposed to be—he needed to think he was not beholding to anyone and to move on with what he thought was his agenda! He has performed well thinking he was his own person.

Now that Mr. Obama is President, TWCTW are moving to the next phase of their plan. To assure the Democrats remain in power, TWCTW created the so-called Tea Party. The TWCTW all congratulated each other at the genius of such a creation. On the surface, it appears to be a maverick social movement devoid of love or affection for either political party—much like the spirit of the membership of TWCTW. It is, however, the enabling force for the continuing perpetuation of the status quo.

After the mid-term elections oust incumbents from both parties, the traditional polarity of Republicans vs. Democrats will be a thing of the past. The battles between the two-party philosophies has always been the smoke and mirrors that keep the public from focusing on the real intentions of TWCTW.

The real question, however, must be what is TWCTW up to? So, here's the deal.

TWCTW have already decided President Obama is going to be a one-term president. Somebody has probably already taken him aside and explained the reality. He was the best candidate to unplug the power cord to the Bush Republican political machine. Having accomplished that feat, it was still no easy task to get some of the major social legislation through Congress in Obama's first two years—probably because TWCTW had to work with Nancy Pelosi and Harry Reid and a Congress where civility did not extend across the aisle.

TWCTW know that they have exhausted the political currency of the Democratic Party through the ethos of President Obama. His feet have turned to clay. That's where the Tea Party comes into the picture.

When the smoke clears Congress will be in disarray. Nancy Pelosi will be history—as will be Harry Reid—not because they deserved to be ousted, but because it is time for change.

Ironic, but TWCTW are going to make a second run at the Presidency using the rhetoric of change. This time, however, they have decided that it is time to move Secretary of State Hillary Clinton to center stage.

President Obama will voluntarily step aside and be the most magnanimous President in history. He will choose to move on to another life that will produce for him the same kind of wealth afforded President Bill Clinton. The lucrative speaker's and book promotion circuits beckon. He will accrue far more personal wealth in the four years following his one-term Presidency than he can currently imagine. He will also relish his family life and not put it on hold for four more years. And he won't have the headaches associated with being President.

Think about the appeal. The Democrats move on after the mid-term defeat. They now position the well-trained in international relations Hillary Clinton to become another social first—the first woman president. Whoever she runs against from the Republican Party will be throwing stuff at Teflon. She will be better than an incumbent. Nothing will stick. Good strategy TWCTW! That's why you are in control of everything!

Hillary Clinton will be able to distance herself from the Obama agenda and not have to disavow it. She will connect with a powerful female vote and not have to defend health care, a war policy, or a domestic economy that has not been performing as the Democratic Party would like. The theme will be simple. I will give you a kinder, gentler Democratic party—the first party to have the female gender! Awesome!

If there is any lesson to be learned in this upcoming election it is this: as preposterous as this conspiracy theory scenario seems, it is just as illogical as any of the multitude of reasons people are going to use to vote out incumbents—regardless of their political records. People who don't think when they make decisions about politicians deserve what they get!

Did I say that was the political motto of TWCTW?

5

"A Defining Moment Decision"

Everyone has an opinion and legitimate standing to express it in the public debate about the recent prisoner swap deal. My standing is as a member of the group of American who did not support candidate Barack Obama for the past two elections. My opinion is that this presidential action will have lasting consequences long after President Obama leaves office. It will overshadow every other positive or negative view of President Obama's leadership. It will become the symbol of Obama Presidential style!

I avoid *ad hominem* attacks on the President. He has a tough job and a desire to succeed. He deserves our respect, even when we strongly disagree with one of his decisions. I want him to succeed. Once elections are over it is time to get on with the business of running the government. I expected our President to focus on the business of government. I expected Congress to cooperate. Sadly, neither the current Administration nor the Congress is meeting my expectations.

When the Affordable Care Act was debated I rooted for the President to take his party's control of both houses of Congress and to initiate a single-payer national health program that would create a system modeled after what I receive as a recipient of Medicare. Sadly, such an option was not selected. Instead, the private insurance industry was retained in its middle-man role.

It is not necessary to resurrect many of the initiatives for revitalizing the economy that did not come to fruition under the President's administration. Cash for Clunkers, the Stimulus program for *"shovel ready"* projects, and the investment in "green" industries didn't pay the dividends envisioned. Our national debt continues to climb out of control.

I am a realist. I know how the best-laid political plans and dreams come and go with each Presidential administration. I know we have gridlock. I blame both parties, not just President Obama. Certainly the current administration has its hands full of issues like immigration and security of our borders.

It wasn't until the President's decision to exchange one American prisoner for five terrorists in our captivity that many Americans experienced the proverbial *"straw that broke the camel's back."*

The camel's back is the spirit we have in America that takes pride in our form of government and the role we play as a leader throughout the rest of the world. We cherish our Constitutional form of government that integrates the roles of the executive branch with the legislative and judicial branches.

It was frustrating to learn the President "went it alone" without Senatorial support in engineering the prisoner swap. He felt he was doing the right thing—based on his intelligence that the prisoner was in failing health—and his fear that revealing we were negotiating the exchange was going to result in the enemy killing their prisoner. In his mind time was of the essence—and secrecy was paramount.

I don't share the view that he violated the law. As our Commander-In-Chief he had the power to make his decision. There are circumstances in which he can circumvent Congress. And, in the months ahead I expect him to put the best political spin on his decision as he continues to experience pushback. And, one thing is certain—pushback will come from all parts of our political spectrum. His decision is a defining moment decision that will produce debate for years to come as politician's align or distance themselves from the decision and historians write about Obama's legacy.

There are things a Commander-In-Chief must do that do not warrant anything but getting on with the messy business of ending American's involvement in what has proven to be its longest war. However, he should have resisted the temptation to try and milk the politics of prisoner exchanges like he did with the soldier's parents in the Rose Garden.

In retrospect, one has to wonder why our President— knowing as he must have surely known about the curious circumstances surrounding the soldier captivity—placed a high priority on championing the lopsided exchange. The decision speaks volumes about Obama's personal agenda—not the American people's agenda.

Why didn't our President do what would have been consistent with his view. Get the soldier home at all costs—and irrespective of his alleged deserter status—and simply let the military justice system run its course? Why stage the Rose Garden theatre?

That's my beef in this Presidential decision. It is appalling that once again a spokesperson for the administration put the spin that *"the soldier served with honor and distinction."* Under the circumstances, such spin-doctoring greatly diminished the public perception of the President's integrity.

If the war against terrorism were a war of territorial boundaries, then certainly leaving Afghanistan would have warranted the swap of prisoners. However, the war against terrorism is not about geopolitical boundaries. Exiting Afghanistan does not signal the end of war—these five prisoners are now free to conspire again and kill

Americans. In their mind the war continues. It is a war of ideologies not a war of military might!

The lop-sided exchange is an American diplomatic tragedy. It saddens and demoralizes many Americans. It will undoubtedly be one of the singular events of the Obama presidency that will stir up continuing debate as the mid-term elections and the 2016 Presidential election heats up—and will remain controversial long after President Obama leaves office.

6

"A Pox on Both Houses'"

No one should be surprised at the vote on Wednesday in which the House voted overwhelmingly to overturn the year-old piece of health care legislation—dubbed by many in the unmerciful rhetoric of the public forum as "Obamacare."

Make no mistake about what the vote represented. The vote wasn't about how to further improve our system of health care delivery or how to improve the quality of services it provides patients. The vote wasn't about eliminating the billions of dollars of fraud and waste in the current system. It wasn't about bringing more people into the health care system that previously had no coverage. It wasn't even about validating the true cost of the current legislation.

What was the vote about? It was about political symbolism. It was a throwing down of a gauntlet. The

Senate will undoubtedly not support the House vote—but that is expected. Politicians on both sides of the aisle are simply setting the stage for the upcoming 2012 Presidential campaigns. In the unlikely event the Senate goes with the House vote, President Obama has no alternative but to veto the bill. The vote was about Washington political partisanship. It was not an indicator of Congress' genuine concern for the health status of the American people.

Where does that leave us who were viewing the current Federal legislation as the first solid step in the direction of some form of universal health care coverage? For many it leaves us with a bad taste in our mouth and the temptation to shake our heads in disgust and mutter *"a pox on both houses."*

Let me repeat: the vote wasn't about health care—sadly. It was about politics. Those who rely on the government for health care entitlements, or upon government to regulate insurance so people can afford private insurance, are being told that the expansive plan the Obama administration got past Congress in its landmark legislation was a mistake. It was something the people didn't want and the dissatisfaction with the law led to the overwhelming defeat of the Democratic Party in the 2010 mid-term elections. The fact that the American people are split almost evenly on support or non-support for the current law does not justify either party throwing out the legislation as un-workable. The challenge is to move forward and modify it so it will work as intended.

The partisan political solution is simple: throw out the baby with the bathwater. Reject the current law foundation and start anew. But, don't really start anew until we have used the health care reform rhetoric to stake out the Democratic and Republican parties political positions in the upcoming elections.

Which party is going to address the reality of where we are with improving health care for the American people? Is improving health care for the American people now relegated to a senseless political game that is really about which party will win the Presidency in 2012? I am cynical and I conclude "yes."

It won't matter if someone like Representative Pete DeFazio of Oregon provides a workable alternative to those who don't want to be told they must purchase health insurance. He wants such folks to be requiring to give-up entitlement to Medicaid in the event they need health care coverage. It is a thoroughly reasonable solution, in my mind.

It won't matter if some creative legislator finds a way to continue the inclusion of people with prior-conditions when it comes to obtaining or retaining health insurance.

It won't matter if coverage of family members is still mandated for insurance companies to include in family coverage until age 26.

It won't make any difference whether someone in the Congressional Budget Office revises cost assumptions and moves the price tag up or down for whatever new policy is proposed by the Democrats.

Sadly, the reality is that both parties realize health care policy will be the defining issue of the upcoming Presidential campaign. The Republicans will use the current House rejection of the health care reform bill as evidence our government is spending too much on health care. Where were these folks when war spending heaped huge debt upon the American people?

We afford wars but somehow balk at affording the "Obamacare" version of national health care. The Democrats will struggle to salvage as much as possible of their landmark legislation—but right now those who assess political strategies say the Republicans have the Democrats "on the run."

The Republicans believe they can use the health care issue as one that will either cause Obama not to seek a second term, or, should he chose to run again, it will be an unpopular position he will be forced to defend.

There is some irony in the fact that when President Bill Clinton ran for his second term of office, he didn't have to defend his health care legislation. It failed to gain the necessary congressional support and died on the floor of Congress, never to re-surface in the presidential campaign. President Obama legislation passed—only to become a seeming albatross around the Democratic candidate's neck in the 2012 election campaign.

As a retired healthcare administrator, I viewed the cumbersome Health Care Reform law that Congress passed as a remarkable step in the right direction. In view of what happened on Wednesday, I say *"a pox on both houses."*

Having vented my frustration, I hope I am wrong and that Congress will truly focus on doing the right thing with health care reform and making the necessary modifications of the current law and fashion bi-partisan compromises to assure our health care is not sacrificed for political expediency.

7

"A Problem On the Horizon with the Affordable Care Act"

It should be crystal clear that a lot of tweaks need to be made to the Affordable Care Act before it officially gets underway this coming October when people access health care exchanges to qualify for government subsidized health insurance. Anyone who has checked into the Cover Oregon website and used the calculator to determine for themselves how much subside they will qualify for to get insurance in Oregon knows this is a step in the right direction to make insurance affordable.

However, the purpose of this article is to explain that the good intentions of the plan as it was hastily conceived and passed through Congress still has some major issues to resolve.

Specifically, we need to distinguish between getting insurance coverage and getting health care access.

Here is the problem, in a nut shell.

Let's presume that an uninsured person wants to use the exchange to get coverage for the whole family. Let's presume that what was heretofore unaffordable is now within the budget of a family. Let's presume that the head of the household signs-up for the coverage. And, somehow a bona fide insurance card is issued to the family.

Now, the issue shifts to understanding how being insured is different from having access.

The Affordable Health Care Act is designed to provide coverage. Sadly, it doesn't follow that insurance coverage mean health care access.

Just because a formerly uninsured individual and family now has an insurance policy doesn't mean there is a health care provider who will accept that person as a patent.

How much shortfall do we currently have in Oregon as far as the capacity of our medical care system is concerned?

Given the shortage of primary care physicians in Oregon, as well as other states across the country that are expanding coverage as a result of the Affordable Care Act, the expanded coverage doesn't solve the issue of the shortage of health care providers.

This is where the plot thickens. What happens if a now insured patient needs health care and cannot connect with a primary care physician?

When a medical issue arises the now insured patient will have no choice but to choose the most expensive alternative—the emergency room at their local hospital. In effect, if there are no primary care physicians willing to accept them as patients because their practices are overflowing with patients, then where does the now insured patient turn for medical care? Emergency Rooms!

However, when the preliminary actuarial studies were made for the Affordable Care Act about having virtually everybody insured, it was argued the hospitals would have substantially less "bad debt" as a result of "no pay" patients seeking emergency care at hospital emergency departments.

Hospitals saw the Affordable Care Act as a major financial benefit because it would reduce the burden of non-paying patients seeking care in emergency departments. Hospitals envisioned how the law would provide them great financial relief—and as a result, understood the rationale that they should receive less payment for government sponsored patients.

My curiosity arises as to whether we calculated the financial consequences of covering most people with affordable health care insurance and left them on their own to find a health care provider for their primary care?

It would appear that hospital emergency departments, instead of getting some kind of relief are now going to get under the current structure of the Affordable Care Act a huge influx of **insured** patients using the ER as the only alternative they have to health care services.

As a former hospital administrator, I wonder how will hospitals deal with this new reality?

Will hospitals tell insured patients they cannot present themselves to emergency departments for what are determined, after the fact, to be primary care, non-emergent medical problems?

Will emergency departments have to re-structure themselves to accommodate non-emergent insured patients?

Will emergency departments have to advise non-emergency patients that their insurance policy acquired through the Oregon Health Care exchange does not allow them to get primary care services through hospital emergency departments.

Now, here is where I switch hats and take the role of the formerly un-insured person and family.

I have primary care insurance. I can't get a provider. But I am now insured! What do I do when we have a medical problem? We no longer have to wait until it is truly an emergency, perhaps life threatening condition. We can present ourselves at the local hospital emergency department and show our insurance card! Let them decide how to bill the government and our co-payment!

How much does it cost to be seen at a local ER for a non-emergency situation compared with an office visit at a primary care physician's office? A no-brainer conclusion! It costs substantially less to see a primary care physician!

So, the bottom line is that the devil is in the detail. How do we make the Affordable Health Care Act work when we don't have the primary care physician network capable of absorbing the new patients? What do we have to do to address this critical dimension of the problem?

Let's figure out this problem sooner rather than later.

8

"BE WARY OF THE *TU QUOQUE* FALLACY"

Many years ago when I taught a course in everyday reasoning and logic as a unit in my Argumentation and Debate lectures at UC Davis I taught students about *Tu quoque* reasoning. It is a Latin term for "you, too" or "you, also." I taught it was a kind of logical fallacy. It was, in effect, an attempt to use the persuasive **appeal to hypocrisy.** In effect, it says, "Don't listen and evaluate the merits of the opponent's argument because he/she is a hypocrite." It shifts the focus from the argument at hand to an attack on the character of the opposing advocate—which I cautioned was a kind of *ad hominem* argument. I taught it was an argument that attempts to discredit the opponent's position by asserting the opponent's failure to act consistently in accordance with the very position he was taking on an issue. *Tu quoque* argument attempts to show that a criticism or objection being made by an opponent applies equally to the person making it. The person who uses *Tu quoque* reasoning is attempting to dismiss an opponent's position on an issue by arguing the person is inconsistent.

I used to diagram the argument as follows:

The advocate (A) makes criticism of a policy or action of the opposition (P)

The advocate (A) is also guilty of such a policy or action (P).

Therefore, P is dismissed.

From a legal point of view, there is a legal maximum that states a person cannot approach the courts of equity with unclean hands. If there is a nexus between the applicant's wrongful act and the rights he wishes to enforce, the court may not grant the applicant's request.

In the International Criminal Tribunal—in the case of the former Yugoslavia when it was accused of crimes, the *Tu quoque* argument was used unsuccessfully. Yugoslavia argued a justification for its crimes by arguing the opposing side had also committed such crimes.

Interestingly enough, at the Nuremberg trial of Karl Donitz *Tu quoque* argument was accepted not as a defense of the crime itself, or to the prosecution proceedings, but as a defense only to punishment.

Bottom line, not all use of *Tu quoque* arguments involve logical fallacy. One convenient and not fallacious way to use such argument is to point out the similarities between the activity of the opponent and the activity about which he is questioning. However, to label the opposing advocate as something—a hypocrite—does not excuse the advocate of his own inappropriate action.

I raise these old lecture notes on this occasion because I think we have a classic case in the controversy generated by the Archbishop and the arguments the current Executive Director of Catholic Community Services of Lane County (CCSLC) has used to oppose the Archbishop's directive to sever its relationship with United Way because it associates CCSLC with a known provider of abortions.

In the course of argument, the issue was raised when one argument characterized the archbishop inconsistency in dealing with the support of Regency Insurance company, while at the same time telling the Catholic Community Services of Lane County to sever its relationship with a known provider of abortion by withdrawing from United Way.

The Biblical argument was the classic example in which the caution was given to reconsider being so critical of finding a sliver in someone else eye and not seeing the timber or log in our own eye.

I think the ***ad hominem*** dimension of this argument against the archbishop's position surfaces by using a scriptural quote in an attempt to defeat the argument of someone who is supposedly knowledgeable about scripture—like using his own words against him.

I know I cannot—nor do I wish to change the minority vote in this matter. I respect the thinking of those who argued we should withdraw from being an affiliate of the archdiocese because the Archbishop has been inconsistent with his own behavior.

I do wonder however where those who favored withdrawing from the Memorandum of Understanding with the Archdiocese of Portland would stand today if we made the following suppositions:

- Suppose the archbishop had no dealings with Regency?
- Suppose he had not taken money in any form from the health insurance company that you correctly identify as a source of funding for abortions?
- Suppose he was "free of sin (of inconsistency)" and directed us to sever our relationship from United Way?
- Would we have been willing to remove the "sliver" in our own eye if in fact the Archbishop only had a "sliver" in his eye, or, ideally, no "sliver" at all?

I do not feel the need to hold the Archbishop accountability for consistency in his thinking or reasoning. Just like I don't feel the need to hold those accountable who were in the minority view for using the kind of argument they deployed in their advocacy.

I do respect the reality of the situation the Board of Directors of Catholic Charities of Lane County faced.

We were not voting to protest the inconsistency in the archbishop position.

We were voting to affirm we wished to continue under the sponsorship by the archdiocese and remain sponsored as a Catholic organization.

I do expect to hold the whole Board accountable for moving beyond this argument and accepting the majority decision of the Board.

If anyone wishes to continue the debate with the archdiocese and the Archbishop, then that is a course of action I expect will have to undertake outside the scope of authority of your relationship with Catholic Community Services of Lane County. Thank you all for re-grouping as a Board and focusing on the important issues that face us as we move into the new year.

9

"Why We Can't Discover Truth in Presidential Debates?"

If Plato were alive today he would undoubtedly be busily re-writing his famous 4ᵗʰ Century B.C.E. political philosophic treatise, ***The Republic***. Among other things, his book defined a different kind of political correctness than the sense of the term we over-use in modern politics. It also saw a different role for debate and dialectic than what we experience today.

Is it really possible for American society to discover "truth" and to test the strength of arguments and plans to modify our status quo through our current presidential debate process—or has the process simply become poetry, sophistic rhetoric, and a theatre stage where demagoguery prevails?

The Republic envisioned a society in which "political correctness" was defined as following the strict rules created by a wise Philosopher King. The philosopher-king role was to protect society against all forces that distorted Truth. Anything distorting Truth was political incorrect. Hence, the banishment of poets and rhetoricians from any ideal society. Why? Poets engaged in weaving colorful images of reality. They were intellectual "entertainers" who saw the world in terms of the bi-focal lenses of metaphor. They painted a poetic reality by portraying *"the thisness of a that and the thatness of a this"*—to use literary critic Kenneth Burke's explanation of poetic reality. Rhetoricians—or more precisely, 'sophistic rhetoricians'—engaged in arguments that always *"made the worst case seem the better."*

After listening to the Democratic and the Republican Parties' presidential campaigning foreplay we *"poetically"* call *"debates,"* one can rightly assume Plato would banish all candidates for being some combinations of poet or rhetorician. That would raise the challenge of finding a "philosopher-king" through some other social process.

The goal of our modern Presidential Campaign Theatre is not to discover either truth with a small "t" let along get the public to transcend and discover the Truth with a capital "T" about how to improve American Society and/or the world in which we live.

At its best modern political campaigning is "theatre." It is theatre in the sense a candidate's "ethos" and "pathos" supersede the "logos" or well-reasoned argument. At its worst, it has become "sophistry" in the truest sense of the word—where candidates use rhetoric to make the worst case seem the better.

It is also tempting to introduce another dimension of early Greek culture to describe modern political presidential theatre. It can be likened to early Greek theatre where the audience enjoys the off-center-stage "Greek Theatre Chorus" drone of social media—most notably, Facebook, Tweets, and Twitters—to accompany the center-stage political drama unfolding during the debates. It is this constant stream of political chirping Plato would probably find even more threatening to an ideal society than the presence of poets and rhetoricians.

Many American tuned into social media are bombarded with political messages and well-tailored sound-bites and posters designed to replace critical thinking. Instead of learning how to express personal thougnts and opinions, people simply post and pass on political blurbs and ad hominem attacks and ask friends if they "like" or "agree" to pass it on to others.

Anyone on Facebook for the purpose of sharing personal and family information with friends and acquaintances is inundated with political rhetoric and poetics.

Such a "chorus" of support for candidates might be viewed as providing the electorate with an invitation to participate in the drama by joining the chorus. On the other hand, one has to question whether cut-and-paste arguments replace critical reasoning and independent thinking? It is easier to connect with a media-savvy organization and get pre-packaged arguments. Like sausage in which we don't know the ingredients, the media chorus gives voters cookie-cutter truths and half-truths and lies to attach to their Facebook page and pass on to their friends and family.

In a Platonic ideal society, it would certainly be "politically incorrect" to create a staged drama that pretends to test the veracity of a political position by having a half-dozen candidates on stage constructing sound-bite responses to a moderator's often inane and self-serving questions. The recent Republican debate wasn't testing policies with counter arguments and reasoning in an effort to get at "truth" with a small "t." The Democratic "debate" wasn't much better—though there were fewer players on stage.

We will never have a version of Plato's Republic operating in our modern society—and perhaps that is just as well. We will never have presidential debates using a Platonic dialectic process to probe as best we can the truth and veracity about what will best work to improve our modern political structure we inherited from the early Greek democratic tradition.

We can however, strive to find better ways to determine which non-Philosopher King (Or Queen) is best prepared to lead us toward a better society. Like Plato's world, we are not going to find a philosopher-king (queen) to lead us.

Why not create a true debate climate when two final opposing party candidates focus on a specific debate resolution that allows reasoned analysis and clash of opposing evidence, reasoning, and logic and allow the electorate to truly weigh which position holds the most truth and has the greatest likelihood to produce results?

Maybe the reasons we don't have the candidates engage in true debate is because an electorate is unequipped to evaluate arguments and discern which side is stronger and making the best case. Or, most candidate's are not skilled in the art of debate. Or, as is more probably the case, unwilling to do the hard work of evaluating which argument is strongest.

Maybe that's why modern politicians see the truth as secondary to the tools of sophistry and demagoguery. Maybe that's why the truth can't be discovered in modern presidential debates?

10

"THE MINIMUM WAGE: TAX SOCIETY NOT SMALL BUSINESSES"

I read Jonah Goldberg's Register-Guard April 20, 2016 column entitled *"Minimum Wage Hike Fails on Moral Grounds."* I have a different take on the matter. My problem with the minimum wage is based on something more than "moral grounds." It fails the test of political ethics. The way it is proposed amounts to what I perceive as "politically unethical social engineering," not sound economic theory. It is a welfare "tax" by any other name. The challenge is to determine who should pay it—society or the small business owner?

I vacillated on the topic of minimum wage for decades—having been through the debate about what constitutes a "livable wage" *(which I prefer to call a "livable income")* when I was the Dominican Hospital COO, a major employer in Santa Cruz, CA. I was in a unique position because the lowest wage we paid at the hospital was significantly higher than the proposed "livable wage" advocated by the minimum wage political lobby in the community. I admit such a reality made me less appreciative of the burden raising the minimum wage would have on the small businesses Goldberg cites in his article. Now that I am retired and have lived almost a decade in Eugene, I continue to see the virtue of raising low-wage worker's income, but now see it in a different light.

My thesis is simple. I agree it is virtually impossible for someone earning $10 dollars an hour to survive in our community's economic environment. As a member of the larger society and someone who has compassion for low-income members of our community, I favor assistance to raise the income of the worker. What I object to, however, is what I call "social engineering" done in the form of a government mandated minimum wage. I am a firm believer in having the economy be driven by supply and demand forces—independent of government interference.

For example, if a job has a labor supply of workers willing to work for $10 dollars an hour, then I think the owner of the business must pay the market price or not find sufficient help. If help cannot be secured at the $10.00 per hour rate, then the owner must pay more until the positions are filled. It is understandable that the cost of labor will be included in the price of the product. That is my simple explanation of labor supply and demand as it operates in a business.

I cannot ignore the reality that $10 dollars an hour is insufficient to manage in our economy so I am willing to find other ways to get money into the pocket of the worker. Someone smarter than I arrived at the conclusion that $15 dollars an hour is a "livable income." So, as a community member I agree we should "tax" ourselves and give the low-wage $10 dollar an hour worker a subsidy of $5.00 per hour.

We should clearly identify the subsidy for what it is—a welfare tax on our society to assist low-income earners have a "livable income." The wage-earner should also realize that many in our society—if not the majority— wants people to have a livable income—independent of the economics of labor force supply and demand for a particular job category. As the labor source becomes more scarce, the natural economics will cause wages to increase and presumably the price of the product will increase to support the natural supply and demand equation. As labor becomes scarce, presumable the "tax" burden on the larger community will be lessened.

My objection to government simply mandating the wage that must be paid by the employer is this: Such a policy seems to place the burden exclusively on the business owner to fund the social conscience of the larger community. I don't think that is either "fair" or "moral." The politicians who advocate and enable a $15 dollar an hour minimum wage are in effect "hiding" the "tax" by putting it exclusively on the business. I prefer to get this "tax" out into the open and give the large society both the credit and the corresponding responsibility to fund it. An artificial minimum wage of $15 dollars an hour may earn kudos to the politicians who support it, but it removes from the larger society the burden of paying for this social benefit.

There is a lot of angst among some that our American economy is incrementing itself in the direction of a European-style socialistic economy. If such a reality is in fact coming to pass, then I think we have the responsibility to let the American people see what is happening and not disguise a socialistic welfare-state under the pretense of an artificially inflated wage structure in our economy.

There is nothing wrong with society showing pro-active concern for the economic welfare of its citizens by assuring the lowest-paid employees have a pre-determined "livable income." If that is the equivalent to $15 dollars and hour, fine with me. Of course, the devil is in the detail regarding the best way to structure this tax plan.

In the process of creating the "tax" make sure it is placed on the society as a whole and not the small business owner who is likewise trying to survive. Not to do so is what I perceive as an unethical political gambit designed to disguise a welfare "tax."

11

"Caveats about Change"

I was among those who listened with interest during the past presidential election when candidate Barack Obama engineered his remarkably successful campaign around the promise to bring about "change" in Washington politics. Now that we are a year into the Obama presidency, I think it is appropriate to revisit the whole concept of **change**. Is the call for **change** merely a rhetorical strategy or do we really understand what **change** truly entails?

I recently ran across a collection of aphorisms I created and modified during my career as a member of a hospital organization's leadership team. I was especially struck by how relevant my previous comments about managing change in a complex health care organization appeared to be for those who manage government. I realized, too, that Congress has the power to **decide**, but lacks the power or expertise to **manage** the results of their decisions to change things. Such a reality may be the underlying cause of uneasiness on the part of folks who are inherently distrustful of big government. Here are my observations:

- Change can only be initiated by those who are in power.
- Change is an event—a decision point—not a permanent or lasting outcome.
- Change is not a process, but an event in time we cause; one cannot manage change—one can only manage a process.
- Nobody ought to be rewarded for simply causing change or being a change agent. Any idiot with power can amass quantities of change on his/her resume; the reward ought to go to those who can and do engineer quality outcomes as a result of changes made.
- No organization thrives on change; it thrives on consistency that is flexible enough to modify and create effective processes to bring about improved quality.
- Change what is dysfunctional and nothing else.
- One doesn't 'manage' change; one causes a change that must then be managed.

- Change is sometimes driven by a desire for quality; sadly, it is more often at the expense of quality when it is not effectively managed.
- Change isn't hard if you have power; what is hard is deciding on what changes to make.
- Reducing overhead is often like giving the organization a haircut; it changes the appearance of things for a while, but it doesn't take long for things to look shabby again if change is not managed effectively.
- In any human organism—including government— muscle weighs more than fat. Unfortunately, during the change of downsizing, it is difficult to know the effect on the organization's performance if all we do is weigh the flesh that is on the cutting room floor.
- It is a great act of faith—if not downright folly—to believe one can improve organizational performance by simply adding or subtracting people who operate within a broken system.
- Finding a better way to do something in a complex organization usually requires the discipline of first knowing how it is supposed to work before making a change.
- Most organizational changes are initiated for reasons of economic survival, not out of a quest for improved quality.

- Organizations that understand 'quality' is a verb are apt to better understand the true relationship between quality and change.
- When organizations—especially government organizations—are in need of critical changes, it's usually a sign they don't know how to manage quality.
- The more organizations—especially government organizations—have ignored managing quality outcomes, the greater the need to initiate change.

Those of us who want true health care reform want more than governmental decisions that mandate change. We want a government that understands successful change goes beyond securing the necessary power to pass a bill the President signs. We want a clear design for how the change is going to be managed in a cost-effective manner and how it will meet or exceed customer satisfaction. We want a government that we can hold accountable for managing the processes impacted by Congressional change orders—whether the change is in health care or any other area of government mandated change.

12

"Congress Fiddles While America Flounders"

Whether one is a Republican, a Democrat, or an Independent, there is no denying the American public's frustration with our Congress has reached a low point according to virtually every polling agency. This is not a right-wing Republican diatribe. It is an American lament!

It appears from their actions Congress is oblivious to this voter discontent. Consider this recent piece of evidence. Congress is now fiddling while America is floundering— to paraphrase the often cited metaphor of an ineffective Roman leader's inability to address the real problems of his country. Such fiddling is exemplified by the letter 50 U.S. Senators recently sent to the leadership of the Washington NFL football franchise. In a nutshell, it expresses the view of some Senators that they should use their prestige and political clout to pressure the ownership to relinquish the name "Redskins."

One has to question the priorities when Senators take the time to weigh-in on the issue of whether it is "politically correct" to have the Washington NFL football team retain its eighty-year-old franchise name "Redskins" because some feel it is offensive to Native Americans.

I am neither advocating nor opposing the views of those who think reference to Indians and sports teams at the school level or the professional level is appropriate. Such an issue is not relevant. It is a tempest in a teapot red-herring debate that begs the issue of what Senators should be spending their time debating. I advocate Congress spends its time on the really significant problems facing our country—and not the contrived political issues of judging the appropriateness of the names of professional sports franchises.

My first awareness of this trend occurred in my own hometown of Palo Alto when several years ago Stanford University relinquished its mascot "the Indians" in favor of the more politically correct image of "the Cardinal." I admit it would be hard to fashion a mascot personifying the color "cardinal," but I abhor the silly tree that cavorts on the football field as the visual image of a team mascot. Perhaps Senators could be persuaded to remedy this situation?

I don't fault Senators who felt they could affix their name and prestige to a letter to the ownership of the Washington Redskins NFL football franchise. Politicians have a keen sense of what is political correct these days. Such political awareness, however, begs the issue of whether the action is relevant. I am sure someone will write to justify this Senatorial indignation. Who can object to taking a stand on such a supposed "injustice" as allowing a sports franchise to be so blatantly "racist" and ignore the feelings of some Native Americans Indians.

I am among those American's who did not elect Congress—members of the House or the Senate—to serve as the moral compass and the social referee to judge what is appropriate nomenclature for a sports franchise.

At least there was no accompanying petition that reflected the Senate's preference for a more politically correct name. I suspect if such an issue were debated in Congress we would have gridlock unrivaled in recent years!

I would like Senators and Congressional Representatives to address the real problems in our society. I would like to see efforts focused on what it is going to take to break the cycle of poverty that is affecting far too many citizens.

If you want to discuss the morality of America culture, get beyond the charge that sports franchise names offend some. Where is the outcry for telling young women not to get pregnant while in high school and unmarried?

Where is the outcry to tell young men not to father children when they are not in a position to remain in a family and raise the child?

Where is the outcry to change the funding of education so students can enroll in college and gain the resources to better their lives without accumulating a massive student loan debt that burdens them after graduation and prevents them from entering main-stream economic realities?

If you want to discuss the complexity of the American culture, where is the outcry that challenges our society to reduce the culture of entitlement and to incentivize young folks to develop the habits of delayed gratification and to work and save for a future?

Congress is supposedly the governmental system in which we work as a country to find the creative compromises and means to resolve the main problems facing our country.

Is there anyone reading this article who would dare to say that "the name of sports franchise" should be on the list of Congressional concerns?

As the upcoming 2014 mid-term congressional elections approach, it may be a good time to ask those running for office to clarify whether this current Congressional "fiddling" over sports franchise names is a worthy issue to occupy any Congressional concerns.

There are many in our electorate who are concerned about the declining position America appears to have in our international role as the leader of the free world.

Many are concerned about the need to restructure our tax system so we can truly compete in a global economy.

Many are concerned about finding ways to increase the number of job opportunities for all sectors of our economy.

I suspect, in the grand scheme of things, there are some voters impassioned by the actions of the 50 senators who petitioned the NFL to change the name of the Washington Redskins. I am willing to bet, however, that there are a lot of American Indians who are more concerned with getting opportunities for their children to complete high school, get college or vocational training that leads to real jobs, and get some affordable health care access, than there are those worried about what an NFL franchise calls its team.

It is time to stop fiddling, Congress, and to start finding solutions to the real problems facing our country.

13

"Fixing the Real Problem!"

Whether you are a "Dump Trump" advocate or a "Can Clinton" pro-Bernie Sanders' supporter, a lot of energy is being wasted on our Presidential election—not to mention a sinful sum of campaign finances. Imagine, Jeb Bush squandered over **"100 million dollars"** in his failed attempt to win the Republican nomination! Pundits project the general election will cost both parties in excess of ONE BILLION DOLLARS!

Sadly, we should be looking to fix the system by asking each candidate to support drastic campaign reform—something that is not likely to occur given the status quo of American politics.

As much as we can demonize each presumptive candidate for the baggage they would bring to the office of President of the United States, whoever win in November and occupies the White House will continue to oversee a broken American democracy. The crisis isn't in the miserable choices we have for the top leadership position—our crisis lies in our failure to fix our broken Congressional circumstances. It is a crisis not unlike the one that festered in Britain until the recent Brexit vote!

The recent calamity created in the United Kingdom with the people voting to exit from the European Union signals the British citizens are fed up with the economic and political status quo of their membership in a dysfunctional E.U. It purports to be an "ugly divorce" with world-wide implications.

Everybody got it wrong in their predictions—the economists, the pollsters, the pundits, and the political scientists. The same thing is happening in America with the populist tsunami of the Trump and the Sanders phenomena.

There are those among us who don't want either Clinton or Trump as president. However, many would accept either if we the people had the energy and determination to support a drastic change in the way we fund, elect, and retain politicians.

It would possibly sooth the upset stomachs voters will suffer as they try to digest the outcome of the current presidential selection process IF we knew significant reform could be on the horizon.

We need a referendum vote to accomplish what we cannot expect Congress to fix. Indeed, it is a problem our current Congress representatives and senators do not view as in their best interest to fix. How many senators and congress representatives leave offices millions of dollars wealthier than when they entered? I rest my case—money in politics corrupts.

We need to: 1) limit the funds any candidate can raise to conduct an election campaign; 2) we need to significantly shorten the election campaign cycle by only giving a three or four-month electioneering window to make a case to the voters; 3) we need to elect members of the House and the Senate to one 6-year term—and to eliminate the concept of "incumbent" as no member of either house of congress should have to worry about raising funds for re-election. This should, in effect, eliminate the concept of the professional politician; and 4) we should eliminate the money influence of lobbyists by making it a federal crime to offer or accept post-Congressional tenure jobs or perks for any member of the U.S. House of Representatives of U.S. Senate.

Even though the U.S. Supreme Court upheld the constitutionality of the Citizens United case for unlimited private funding of political campaigns through PACs, We the People can by virtue of the power vested in the referendum or a constitutional amendment make the necessary changes to take the "dark money" out of our political equation. Brits did it! So can we!

Whether one is an Independent, Republican, Democrat, Libertarian, Green Party, or unaffiliated, it is time for the American People to focus on the real problem and change the structure of our political system—and not allow ourselves to get sidetrack in the carnival of demagogic rhetoric that has come to characterize the American political campaigns. We are sick of ad hominem attack and non-policy debates.

The one thing you can be assured of is that this issue is not apt to be on the agenda of any of the current incumbent congressional candidates, or something either political party is apt to include in its campaign platform.

Take heed American politicians, the populist tsunami that just washed over the shores of Great Britain is headed our way!

14

"Political Correctness to a Fault?"

I have no strong feelings regarding re-naming the new Roosevelt Middle School building. What I do have strong feelings about is the rationale for making a name change. I respect the historical accuracy of the information used by the author of the recent Register Guard guest editorial. I understand why the paper did a follow-up news story about the appeal he made at a school forum regarding shortcomings of Theodore Roosevelt and the need to find another more "political correct" modern name for the school.

The whole issue caused me to puzzle over what drove early civic leaders and school board members of the past to select the name in the first place? Was it simply because he was a U.S. President? Were they ignorant of the facts cited in the editorial? Was there some greater reason for selecting the name other than he was a U.S. President? Were there insufficient public facts about this President to warrant the conclusion his name was not going to be an embarrassment to future school children who listened as "historical revisionists" organized different set of facts to portray the character of past presidents?

Anyone who abhors the dastardly deed of the dentist who recently shot the beloved lion in Africa should have sufficient reason to reject the name of Theodore Roosevelt—the great hunter who thought nothing of hunting big game trophies he brought back to the Smithsonian Museum. My point being that someone can always find a legitimate beef about an historical figure and demonstrate that all mortals have "feet of clay." If for no other reason, given my feelings about trophy hunting, I would support re-naming of the school. But then I'm being "politically correct," aren't I?

It wasn't President Theodore Roosevelt who put his name on the school building. He is not at fault for that decision—but to be "politically correct" isn't the bigger story about why the name was selected in the first place? What did it say about the school leaders at the time? Were they knowledgeable about the shortcomings of the President as we learn from the teacher who is advocating change? Perhaps the author of the editorial has misplaced his criticism.

Delving further into the issue of school building naming I am struck by the reality of how in the past heyday of school constructions after WWII a lot of schools were named for prominent males. Depending on the geographic section of the country I venture to say there are a lot more

Booker T. Washington school names in certain regions than there are Martha Washington school names.

In order to be absolutely "politically correct" in these modern times, shouldn't we go back and have each community create an inventory of its school namesakes. Each community should be given a couple of decades to make sure there is parity so that half of the schools are names after prominent well-known women and half are named after men.

We all know there currently exists inequity in the balance of gender names for schools. So, where do we start to remedy this politically incorrect situation? Let's look at all the schools that are named after Presidents—but let's make sure we have sufficient dirt on every one as we bring forth the case about racism, sexism, cheating, lying, womanizing, financial scandals, etc.

The advocates who want to change the name of Theodore Roosevelt Middle School have just scratched the surface. Surely there are more than sufficient reasons to be critical of the choices made by past generations of school leaders and civic leaders who took the path of least resistance— without proper vetting—and supported the naming of schools after an American President. So, having resolved the issue about continuing to keep the name of the school after the rascal Roosevelt, what about looking into the past history of other Presidents and using such a rationale to re-name these schools with a prominent female name so we can achieve parity in school naming?

Does that mean a Grover Cleveland school should be re-names because that President fathered a child with his mistress according to recent DNA testing? Does that require us to take down the name of schools called Kennedy because history has ample evidence to support the claim that President Kennedy was a womanizer? What about those schools named Clinton? What about those with the name Eisenhower? Both of these presidents were womanizers and adulterer. So was the other President Franklin Roosevelt who frequented the Warm Springs Georgia spa where he was often seen with his par amour. Or, as much as it is not "politically correct" to point out that the great Black leader, Martin Luther King, Jr., also had a reputation as a womanizer—and look at how many schools bear his name.

So, if we are going to be "political correct" in these modern historically enlightening times and make sure we don't name public buildings after rascals, now is the time to get on with this inventory. If this is going to be the political year when at least one party's Presidential candidate is coalescing the female vote, changing the name of Roosevelt Middle School to a more acceptable female name is not only a step in the right direction of gender equality in America, but it is a time for halting this bad habit of recognizing bad people from getting schools named after them.

Or, is this an example of "political correctness to a fault?"

15

"Presidential Material"

As the Presidential election campaigning season approaches and candidates announce they are putting together an "exploratory committee" to assess support for entering the race, I have strong opinions about what I would like to happen. I believe our political process puts the proverbial cart before the horse. Both parties need to do some homework before we open up the process for applicants.

I take a deep breath and pause when I hear the names Sarah Palin, Donald Trump, Mike Huckabee, Mitt Romney, and scores of lesser know names testing whether they have enough support to warrant launching a serious and expensive Presidential campaign.

My question is not whether these people are qualified to fill the position—but whether we as an electorate have any consensus on what we are seeking? I have not yet decided who I will support—the incumbent or the challenger. I have made up my mind, however, to develop a score card for evaluating the candidates based upon some criteria other than popularity or electability—or on the basis of who makes the most attractive campaign promises. I encourage both political parties to do likewise.

In private industry any large corporation would draft a job description outlining the minimum qualifications for applicants. The description would list specific experiences and background the business wants to know before granting an applicant an interview—e.g., advancing to the presidential primary evaluation period.

If I could tweak our democratic process I would have the two major political parties formulate their own "search committee" before we open the process for "unsolicited" applicants from a wide array of aspiring candidates. Each party should write a job description stating what they are seeking. The criteria should be made public to assist the electorate compare the qualifications of candidates. Candidates should view the Presidential Primary race as the forum in which to demonstrate to the American public---the stockholders in our Democracy--how well they meet their political party's specific criteria.

I know one can argue the US Constitution stipulates the minimum Presidential qualifications: Applicants must be a natural born American citizen who is over the age of 35. The applicant must agree to support the values and governmental rules contained in the US Constitution. That's the description in a nut shell.

It doesn't say "political experience desired" or required. The applicant doesn't have to show a minimum of X years in the US Congress—either the House of Representatives or the US Senate. We don't require any level of education—not even graduation from an accredited college or university. We don't require any law degree. We don't ask applicants to demonstrate evidence of understanding business and economics—or have any business experience even though they are expected to oversee the largest business enterprise in the free world. Sadly, many candidates simply tout whether they know how to work the system to get elected—not whether they are the best qualified to serve once elected.

Without a thoughtful job description that identifies specific qualifications needed by applicants at this moment in our history we rely upon such things as "media appeal" and "personal charisma" and appeal to a particular ethnic segment of the voting population. I don't mean to imply these are not real considerations, but what is it we really need now in the pool of applicants?

Over the years there have been many unspoken criteria that de facto screened-out qualified would-be Presidential applicants. There was no sign in the government's window that said "Whites Only," or "Catholic Irish Need not Apply," or "No Women Need Apply"—but these criteria certainly were political realities we had to overcome in defining modern "Presidential Material."

Surely we are sophisticated enough in our two-party system to articulate the ideal qualifications and experience we are seeking in our quest for a President in the election of 2012.

The incumbent's party should huddle and define what it wants for the incumbent to continue in his role. Once the party has clearly stated its needs, then the party verifies it endorses the incumbent. It then becomes the task of the incumbent in the campaign process to demonstrate how well he meets his party's expectations as measured by the criteria of their job description. Even though it is considered politically incorrect for an applicant in one's own party to challenge the incumbent, if in fact someone within the incumbent's party demonstrates they better meet the party's criteria, then they deserve to make their case in the Presidential primary. We need to abandon the conventional wisdom of the incumbent being de facto the candidate of choice for the party.

I intend to sit down and write out specifically the criteria I will use to evaluate the resumes of all candidates. What kind of successes do I wish candidates to demonstrate in a resume? Do I wish a candidate be a person of religious faith? Do I wish a candidate to have a strong position on the issue of abortion? Do I wish the candidate to have success in foreign relations? Do I want a candidate who has experience in operating a company or a government entity on a budget and has been successful in meeting the budget? Do I want a candidate who understands how to use key success metrics to identify the important things to measure track and hold the government accountable for achieving?

I encourage each voter to do the same thing. I know what I don't want in a candidate: I don't want a media personality—a talking head that is photogenic. I don't want someone who only tests the way the political winds are blowing and who is governed by what political polls indicate will please the majority. I want someone capable of realizing they are applying for the most thankless job in the world—but the most important. Let's take the time to improve our role as voters and hopefully as organized political parties so we can bring to the forefront the most qualified applicants who clearly represent our view of "Presidential Material."

16

"Pro-College Football: A Modest Proposal"

When Jonathan Swift wrote in 1729 his **Modest Proposal** he satirized a solution to poverty in Ireland by suggesting citizens consume unwanted children as a source of tasty protein!

The following modest proposal to reform collegiate football will surely be considered absurd by purists. Some will see it as cannibalizing the darling child of American amateur athletics—the so called "student-athlete."

The problem with the status quo is that everybody except the amateur athlete makes money on the business enterprise. We are already eating our young football athletes and not paying a market price for the flesh we are consuming!

It is time to address this inequity. It is time to cannibalize a flawed economic model that has evolved in NCAA Collegiate football. It is time to recognize we have transformed amateur collegiate football into a business enterprise that is driven by "athletes-who-must-be-students" and enrolled in a university instead of the original intent of having "student-athletes" exchange their athletic talents for a full-scholarship leading to an academic degree.

Most Division One football programs place high priority on graduating "student-athletes." The higher the number of graduates the bigger the recruitment boast the program can make. I propose that if we changed the status quo, then such a criterion becomes irrelevant. The success of a program would be measured by how many athletes matriculated to the next level and go on to an NFL team. The really interesting statistic would be the percent of players who actually chose to go to the university where they played on its sponsored club team! Imagine how novel it would be that occasionally a real "student-athlete" would emerge and be championed as an actual student at the sponsoring university!

I love to watch Oregon football. I don't advocate that the University of Oregon stop "sponsoring" a football team—just sponsor it under a different model. Don't require athletes to attend the university. Agree to reformulate the leagues and uncouple teams from the idea they are championing "student-athletes." Call it what it is—a feeder league for the NFL. Pay the market price for the athletes coming from the talent pool created by the nation's high school leagues.

How much would it cost the University of Oregon, for example, to recruit and retain a LaMichael James—or a Darrin Thomas—legitimate Heisman Trophy candidates? How much would Stanford have to pay to retain the services of Andrew Luck?

The status quo of NCAA football at Division One doesn't actually eat its young—it simply subject them to indentured servitude and prevents them from earning a piece of the true economic value they provide the business of Division One NCAA collegiate football.

The case was recently made in the **Register-Guard** that for many of the "student-athletes" on the University of Oregon football team there is indeed an economic quid pro quo—a $30k to 40k a year economic benefit of a full-ride scholarship in exchange for the time they put in on the gridiron and the off-season hours of conditioning and preparation.

In order to initiate a method to level the playing field for all NCAA Division One teams who wished to convert their current program into a new pro-college football league, it would be necessary to have the NCAA role transform into a league model analogous to the NFL. A draft of high school talent would have to be initiated. The athletic departments would prepare themselves for the draft and do as the professional teams currently do in the NFL draft. It would be the league's responsibility to find ways to assure parity and competitiveness among member teams.

There would no longer be the current rules of NCAA recruitment and selection process. Families who want compensation for their talented high school athletes would no longer have to be ashamed of asking for under-the-table, illegal signing bonuses! Universities would not have to play the game of selling families on the virtues of the university's educational program.

NCAA Division One football athletics is the "business/entertainment" subsidiary of the university. Such enterprises have a separate budget, a different pay-scale, and are considered a partner in the University by helping student-athletes achieve their educational goals.

Football is not the "core business" of the university—nor should it be treated as such regardless of the pressures from some alumni. In order to separate the educational mission from the entertainment subsidiary of the university we need to sever the football program from any pretense it exists for the purpose of allowing gifted athletes to acquire a college degree in exchange for sharing their athletic talents on the college gridiron.

It is time to move forward and agree that we will finally consume the dysfunctional ideal of the "student-athlete" and enjoy creating a University of Oregon sponsored pro-team that all alumni and future alumni who are football fans can enjoy saying "that's the pro-team the University of Oregon" is proud to sponsor.

It is time for such a modest proposal to get serious consideration. It is time we stop consuming for free the flesh of our collegiate athletes and provide them a piece of the action they justly deserve.

17

"Putting a New Limit on the Nation's Credit Card"

I had a strong reaction to the editorial opinion published in the Register-Guard Sunday July 17h by Professor Helen Popper—associate professor of economics at Santa Clara University. Her article cautioned readers about supporting a Constitutional Amendment to require a balanced budget.

I don't know if such an amendment is the solution—or how difficult it would be to enact! But my reaction to her perspective was that she was off-target in focusing on the federal budget; the issue is our nation's credit-card limit!

I had mixed feelings about the perspective Professor Popper used in comparing the debt management of an individual family with the debt management of the federal government. Family credit-card debt has its own mortality—and it is time to affirm the same reality for our government.

My criticism of Popper's perspective is that she makes her point by comparing the importance of debt in a family and used it to support the case that a similar logic applies to our federal government's debt. The government may be generally likened to a family in the sense it must deal with choices to assume debt—but if we are going to make such analog comparisons we need to look critically at how the government is different from an individual family unit. We also need to look at another analogy that makes such a comparison more relevant.

Families are different than governments. Families are mortal and have a life-cycle in which they must grow and take on debt so they can build and develop. Ideally, a successful family meets its debt obligations, accrues wealth, pays down its debt, and in the years of retirement enjoys a debt-free existence where one draws from savings and pensions and social security entitlement and if there is something left over, it is passed on to future generations.

Yes, such a family debt-management cycle is becoming far less a reality for more and more families as they struggle in today's economy and deal with massive credit-card debt management! And, of course, such a debt-free future has disappeared for our nation as we have accrued over $40,000 dollars of long-range debt for ever American!

Governments, however, are entities that perceive themselves as exempt from the rules governing debt for mere mortals. The government can and does take on a different kind of debt—a debt that transcends the lifetime of individual humans and families.

It isn't about the fact both families and government need to manage debt. The problem is that the government—like any responsible family unit—should not have access to a credit card that has no limit. It doesn't make sense for a family and it doesn't make sense for a government—but for significantly different reasons.

To illustrate my point, what incentives would an individual family have to pay off a mortgage or a debt if it knew it could simply pass the obligation forward indefinitely? Why pay off the balance of any credit card? Why not enjoy instant gratification and purchase anything one desired? That is the sad state of affairs we find with our current government appetite for charging now and passing debt obligation forward as though the government is immortal when it comes to credit debt.

I am not an economist—but I am someone who is always cautious when it comes to critical thinking. Professor Popper is far more qualified that I am to comment on our current national economic picture. But I don't think her argument contributed much enlightenment to the current credit problem.

If you were to ask me if I am in favor of putting a limit on the national credit card I would say "absolutely." Do I balk at realizing it must be raised beyond its current limits?

Sure. And it goes without saying I would like this to be the last time we increase the limit.

If you asked me, however, "what should that limit be?" I don't have any sophisticated answer. That will clearly be the source of much heated debate as we approach the drop dead date of August 2, 2011! We must raise the limit, but we must also find ways to limit future spending. In a family setting, we would sort between the "wants" and the "needs."

We know that since the creation of our credit-card driven economy we have developed individual habits of indulging in instant gratification instead of saving and paying as we go along. Such a credit-card mentality makes it difficult to educate future generation of family households from developing good credit management habits. The *"buy now pay later"* mentality has thoroughly infected the spending mentality of Congress.

I don't disagree with Professor Popper's conclusion that we don't always have to have a balanced budget—or with her conclusion that balancing a budget in hard times could make downturn worse.

I can't argue with her hypothesis that a balanced budget amendment doesn't put any obligation on Congress to manage spending during good times. I am among those who want significant cuts in spending and in getting the greatest value for what we spend.

Dr. Popper is off target in comparing family economics with government economics. Government is a "corporation" that has a lifespan that transcends the mere mortality of a human life and an individual family's economy.

Unlike a family economy where responsible couples develop a financial plan designed to pay down debt and leave the family debt free during its retirement years, the government can postpone worrying about debt because it suffers from the illusion it is immortal. It is time to hold our government accountable for its own credit-card mortality! Make this the last increase in our national credit-card limit—and focus on living within our means as a government! You, know, like we are on the same page economically as a national family!

18

"Re-Defining the Political Meaning of *Entitlement*"

The current debate regarding raising the national debt ceiling is going to require Democrats and Republicans to re-define the political meaning of **entitlement**. The Random House Webster's Collegiate Dictionary defines **entitlement** as the right to guaranteed benefits under a government program.

There was a time in American culture when we talked about "welfare" and in so doing the concept garnered a pejorative sense—a stigma was associated with welfare because people equated it with a government hand out. The tradition of rugged individualism and self-sufficiency and being responsible for one's own well-being gave way to the realities that the modern economy was not a level playing field for all players. The movement away from the security of a farm and/or a family business in an agrarian culture into an industrialized urban settlement created unique problems for struggling Americans looking for ways to support and grow families.

When our parents and grandparents faced the economic realities of the Great Depression many people felt ashamed of being "on the dole" and having to swallow their pride and accept money from the government to make ends meet to raise their family. Few people saw such funding as being "entitlement" and even fewer wanted to remain on the dole any longer than necessary.

The term "entitlement" softened the reality that government programs had any stigma. With the expansion of government over the past several decades, countless "welfare" programs have permutated into "entitlement" programs—and as a society we have learned to accept this growing segment of our American socially-engineered economy as a necessary reality.

I am an American socialized into believing that "entitlement" is separate from "need."

I am also a retired person over sixty-five and "entitled" to both Medicare and Social Security benefits.

I confess I took early retirement Social Security benefits at age 62. Why? Because I feel "entitled" to the $1600 dollars a month I get from Social Security—and I was worried if I didn't sign up, I would lose this "entitlement" I had **earned**.

Now I introduced a new term, "**earned**." That concept makes "entitlement" much more acceptable for folks like me. If you **earn** an entitlement, it is quite compatible with the American cultural concept of individualism. Sadly, with the exception of Social Security and Medicare, there are few "entitlement" programs that one earns.

I earned (paid into the fund) my social security benefit and therefore I am entitled to it. Period.

Such thinking must be modified. It is time to ask me, do I "need" my social security benefit? If I do, then fine, let the entitlement program send me a check. If I don't meet a means test, then stop payment. That is a reality many of us middle-class and above recipients of social security must come to terms with if we wish to help America survive through these difficult economic times.

Stepping away from Social Security entitlement, I need to look at my Medicare "entitlement" as well.

I want to have health care insurance. When I was employed I paid a portion and my employer paid a portion of the cost of a comprehensive, standard insurance policy. When I retired, I transitioned to a government "entitlement" program Medicare and a supplemental insurance that allowed me to continue with the same type of coverage I enjoyed as a privately insured insurance enrollee.

I think we have approached the point in the American economic model where we also have to ask Medicare entitled patients to meet a means test to determine how much the individual must pay and how much must be borne by the government. Medicare must be based on needs and not on entitlement. This is going to be a major cultural transformation that will be hard for some Americans to accept.

I also am a great advocate of requiring anybody covered by Medicare benefits to participate actively in managing their own health status. If a person is unwilling to participate in pro-actively managing their health care risks and subsequent intervention care protocols, I advocate they should not be considered part of the solution because they choose to be part of the problem for the rest of us tax-payers who are footing the bill for some form of universal health care coverage.

These are extraordinary times that require each American to stop saying they are entitled to something when the reality of our current economic situation is such that we must all make new covenants if we wish the system to work for all of us in the future.

There are many of us who may well be "entitled" to Social Security and Medicare benefits—but we may need to make an additional sacrifice for the common good of our entire society. My only concern is that we find tools to means test that are equitable and spread the responsibility to make sacrifices across the entire spectrum of the American people. I don't want to make the sacrifice if others don't follow suit.

I don't want us to become a society like what we see in Greece. If everybody is entitled to virtually everything, then there is no challenge or opportunity for anyone to use their unique gifts as an individual and acquire wealth and prosperity that is the cornerstone of a capitalistic economy. Sadly, governments can build dependency on government by creating an "entitlement" mentality because it cultivates a dependency mentality.

Let us equate entitlement with "need" and get away from the concept that entitlement can be "earned." Let us stop making people dependent on government for things they should do for themselves. We can no longer afford entitlement programs in their current form.

19

"Re-engineering a Community Newspaper"

Each time I see a national news story about the demise of another newspaper I cringe and wonder how long it will be before I read that the **Register Guard** has been sold to some news conglomerate; or, worse still, is winding down and going out of business. In the two years since I re-located back to Eugene I have seen the newspaper exhibit all of the tell-tale signs of a paper struggling to survive. I've seen it lay-off employees and change the print format in an effort to economize and maintain profitability. I remain impressed with how well the paper provides high quality journalism, despite the economic challenges. I am skeptical, however, that it is just a matter of time until the day of demise arrives. That's why I think it is important to plan ahead and talk openly about ways we as a community could help re-engineer and revitalize our local newspaper. Let's not wait until it is too late to begin such dialogue.

It is time to question whether any community newspaper—including our **Register-Guard**—can continue to prosper in the current business environment.

Indeed, it may be time to explore how we can relieve this important community resource of the burden of operating as a for-profit business. It is time to explore what it would take to convert the enterprise to a community-owned 401 non-profit community benefit organization.

Before you write me off as a radical socialist/communist who advocates public control of private enterprise, allow me to cut you off at the pass. I admire the long tradition of family proprietary ownership that has been the foundation of the **Register-Guard** newspaper. I imagine the Alton Baker family has made a good living operating the newspaper as a profitable business. I imagine, too, they have shared their prosperity with the community in many ways. I am a realist, however, who questions how long one watches the slow-death of many newspapers before one re-assesses whether they want to continue in a business that can no longer earn a return on investment using a traditional business model.

I am aware of the tremendous pressure the internet and electronic media place on the revenue sources of an independent newspaper. Like many newspaper subscribers, I spend a great deal of my time connected to the internet and the instant coverage it provides about national and world events. The evening news coverage of national and world events is often a re-cap of information I have already gleaned from the internet throughout the day.

The same can be said about national and international news that is collected by the editors of the **Register-Guard** and displayed on the morning newspaper. In short, I don't need to have a daily newspaper to inform me about national and international events. It is only occasionally a newspaper story adds to the information I have already obtained hours earlier on the internet.

I do rely on the newspaper for local information. That is the market niche that is most important for me. I want to see the coverage of local sports—high school and college. I want to read about local economy, local political issues, and local events and local personal interest stories. Of course, the trend is to have less and less column inches of these local stories and more and more stories from the national news services.

Even though I can't imagine all the political and economic challenges involved in converting a for-profit newspaper business into a not-for-profit 401 community benefit organization, I have no doubt it could be accomplished.

It is much easier for me to imagine the potential benefits that could accrue: more local journalism, more job security for all involved in the enterprise, more community involvement in assuring the newspaper focuses on the information needs of the local community, and more community pride in preserving an important community resource.

I would remind readers that a not-for-profit organizational model does not mean that the newspaper would cease to sell advertisement or operate so there were excess revenues. It means the paper's "profit" would accrue so a community-based board of directors would decide how best to reinvest the resources to improve the quality of the newspaper. Excess funds could and should be used to encourage the development of young journalism students from the university. The not-for-profit status of the organization would allow the paper to receive donations and grants from foundations and funds that wish to support the growth and maintenance of a strong independent-based community newspaper.

Eugene has always been a town noted for its forward thinking. Perhaps Eugene could become a role model for showing the rest of the country there is a way to preserve high-quality local journalism in the modern information era. I wonder what it would take to initiate such conversation?

20

"An Alternative to Collective Bargaining for Public Employees?"

Jonah Goldberg's RG article on **Union Busting in Wisconsin** (Thursday, February 24, 2011) made an argument explaining what he believes is a distinct difference between private-sector union battles with non-government business owners over employee "fair share" of profits, and public employee unions negotiating with agencies responsible for overseeing the public service funded by tax monies.

I am mulling over whether I buy his distinction. Of course his argument is colored by his belief President John F. Kennedy was politically motivated to strengthen the campaign funds Democrat candidates through such a decision. I am sure in the weeks ahead much will be written supporting and opposing Goldberg's perspective.

I hesitate to weigh in on this topic because of the mixed feelings I have about unions and unionization. My health care administration career began in 1974, the year the National Labor Relations Board (NLRB) ruled in favor of allowing health care employees to unionize. I never felt unions were "good" or "bad." I was taught unions played a positive role in shaping the American work-force. I was also taught unions were either "necessary" or "not necessary"—depending on the condition of the work-place and the quality of the organization's management and its relationship with employees.

I was vulnerable to the mythology that if employees unionized it was a sign of poor management. Such an argument did little except polarize anxious administrators into getting behind anti-union campaigns when a union collected sufficient interest cards to warrant an NLRB election.

For over two decades, I saw what amount to hundreds of millions of dollars spent on consultants who instructed hospital management teams across the health care industry how to wage effective anti-union campaigns when unions like the now well-established Service Employees International Union (SEIU) focused on the huge un-represented population of health care employees.

Perhaps it was fitting that as my career approached its end, the new President of my not-for-profit health care system (Catholic Healthcare West—a 40 hospital system based in San Francisco) decided to initiate a policy of not waging anti-union campaigns when SEIU or any nursing union raised sufficient interest among one of its hospital's staff to warrant an election. It was a radical change from traditional policy. Many old guard administrators felt the company had simply paved the way for the inevitable time when unions would take advantage of hospitals and financially run them into the ground. Such a prediction has not come to pass—though I am sure at least a few would say the jury is still out.

My administrative experience was only with collective bargaining in the **private sector**. On several occasions, my hospital organization went to the brink of strike-preparation with SEIU and the California Nurses Association (CNA) as we prepared to bring in temporary workers until the collective bargaining dispute could be resolved.

I have to admit that collective bargaining—however hostile and antagonist it became—eventually produced a compromise decision between union and management—sometimes through the help of a mediator or an arbitrator. Collective bargaining serves a purpose, even though I look at the financial impact the strong SEIU and CNA presence has on the health care economy of California—as evidenced by the fact a full time benefitted dishwasher in my old hospital can earn in excess of $50 thousand dollars annually. A non-specialized nurse approach and in some cases exceed the $100,000 mark. Such wages and benefits must be put into the California the cost of living perspective.

But the cost of labor is only one dimension of the health care finance problem. I also grimace when I read the CEO of the not-for-profit system—a highly talented leader—earns in excess of $6 million dollars annually. Such a fact simply points to the incredibly complex financial, and some would say imbalance in the so-called not-for profit healthcare financial maze. But that reality must be resolved as a part of the other major national debate on health care policy.

In light of my private sector union experience, I now puzzle over whether collective bargaining with public employees is any different. I'm not sure whether Goldberg is overly simplistic when he asserts that *"government unions negotiate with friendly politicians over tax-payer money, putting public interests at odds with union interest. "*

If the Wisconsin political battle is about eliminating the right of public employees to collectively bargain, then my question is this: "Is there really a viable alternative to collective bargaining for public employees? What is it? What did Jonah Goldberg mean when he said *"Government workers were making good salaries in 1962 when President Kennedy lifted . . .the federal ban on government unions. Civil service regulations and similar laws had guaranteed good working conditions for generations."*

I have long felt that in California (I can't speak for the pattern in Oregon) the tax-payers are to blame for the inflated cost of the PERS benefits. Instead of paying a market-competitive price for labor in the current economy, those who represent the tax-payers balanced annual budgets by withhold wage and salary increases with the promise of a richer contribution to a defined benefit retirement. Those who represented tax payers simply pushed forward the problem. The problem was not "collective bargaining"—it was how the tax-payers were represented in such a process. I do not fault any PERS retiree for becoming frustrated when someone threatens to take away something they have earned as entitlement. I am open to changing the deal for new folks, but not take-away from those who in good faith accepted a bargained contract.

So, to return to what I think is the question of the day, "Do we really have a viable alternative option to collective bargaining for public employees? " Should there be? If so, what is it?

21

"The Difference between Political and Financial Correctness"

When I first relocated to Eugene, Oregon almost four years ago, I was impressed with the new facility that was preparing to open at Sacred Heart Riverbend facility in Springfield. I had a special fondness for the old facility now called the "University District" hospital because my oldest son was born in the facility when I was in graduate school at the University of Oregon in 1967. I think Sister Monica was one of the women religious working in the office to whom I gave my check when my son was discharged to home!

I was stunned at the state-of-the art facility developed at Riverbend. One of my first guest opinion editorials I wrote for the Register-Guard was a piece in which I commended the sisters for having the vision to create a 100-year plan. I chastised those who felt it was too extravagant. I reminded the critics they should be thankful the hospital was re-investing local health care profits in the local community instead of moving them to another venue where the health care system could maximize profits.

My decades of hospital experience, however, caused me to be suspicious of any plans to keep the old University District hospital open once the Riverbend facility was opened and fully operational. It did not make sense, financially, to spend huge dollars to keep acute care at the aging facility.

I had lunch with Mel Pyne, then the CEO of Peace Health, and queried him about the plans to renovate the old facility. I had a similar dilemma at the hospital where I worked in Santa Cruz when we acquired the failing competitor hospital that was located a mile and a half from the main hospital campus. We chose to use the old facility for non-acute inpatient services and outpatient services and consolidated all in-patient services on the main hospital campus.

As I expected, there was a long history of political controversy in which some lobbied strongly that the proximity of the hospital in the University District was critical to assuring Eugene residences they would have access to health care without making the trip out to Riverbend. I realized that for emergency care from most sites in the city of Eugene the connection with the beltline made a trip to Riverbend a direct linkage. I have not seen any studies that show increased risk because of need to be transported to Riverbend instead of University District hospital.

If there was only a financial model driving the decision of what to do with the University District Hospital, it would be a no-brainer decision. Do something else with the old site other than resurrecting its ability to continue to provide emergency and acute in-patient care.

I think it is no coincidence that Peace Health has once again asked for an extension on its plans to renovate the old facility. I appreciate the fact that the Peace Health University District hospital has a negative 26% operating margin, compared with Riverbend hospital's 4.78 percent operating margin. I realize that Peace Health's current financial position is stretched to the point that several of the top executives have exited from the organization— because of work elsewhere or because of internal politics. The new management team—however tentative until a new CEO can be located—must deal with the reality I suspect few want to confront—namely, resist doing the politically correct thing and duplicating acute-impatient services in the University District because of political pressure rather than doing the financially prudent thing and fully integrating all volumes of acute inpatient services to the expansive campus at Riverbend where there is more than sufficient capacity and surrounding space to add services and to increase inpatient bed capacity as the regional demand dictates.

At some time in the future, someone at Peace Health is going to have to bite the bullet and simply confront the reality. It does not make any financial sense to operate two acute-care inpatient facilities serving the same service area. It certainly makes political sense—but it will raise the voice of the community that is unsympathetic with the costs of managing the facility.

Why should the general public care about the operating margin of Peace Health? It will be a celebrate cause if the large, powerful health care provider can be characterized as someone who is making a financial decision that puts the profits of the hospital above the wishes and desires of part of the community it serves.

I do not fault those who advocate for the "politically correct" decision. But I caution those who do to realize that such an action adds significant debt to an organization that is already distressed financially due to a variety of factors—not the least of which is servicing the debt of the new facility and absorbing the expense of maintaining duplicate services at two facilities in the same marketplace.

I am willing to say the "unspeakable" and raise the politically incorrect subject. I think the community needs to support the notion of not rebuilding an acute-care facility on the old University District Sacred Heart site. Find another option that makes sense. Don't unnecessarily duplicate acute in-patient services. It is not in the best interest of the community even though it may appear to be the politically correct decision.

Peace Health at Riverbend is an excellent asset of this community. Don't encumber it with unnecessary debt just to be politically correct.

22

"The Miracle on Pennsylvania Avenue"

I am surprised by two things: none of the political pundits who write nationally syndicated columns that appear in the **Register-Guard** have yet to assert President Obama is going to be successful in securing health care reform legislation—indeed, many remain skeptical. I am also surprised how none have dared to touch the obvious religious allegory in the drama unfolding in Washington these days—perhaps with good reasons: they don't want to raise the dander of the religious right that is already aligned with those who are hopping-mad about the pending health care reform legislation.

As a fiction writer/health care policy advocate, I have shared many strong opinions about the likelihood of successful reform. I am now willing to declare, however, that President Obama will be successful—for reasons that will soon be apparent. I also cannot resist point out the allegory between the events unfolding on Pennsylvania Avenue and the time frame that spans the Christian holidays of Christmas and Easter. Recall it was on Christmas Eve, 2009 when the U.S. Senate stayed late into the evening to give birth to the Senate version of President Obama's health care reform bill. To say the Bill has suffered persecution and scorn from all sides is an understatement. That is why I can't resist the temptation to view President Obama Wednesday evening prime-time speech as his effort to resurrect and prove that there is life after death for the bill that many had abandoned.

Just as it was critical to get the vote before the Christmas break, it is likewise critical to the strategy of the Democrats to get a vote on the revised health care reform package before Congress is dismissed for the Easter break. Critics are upset. They charge such a tactic is clearly designed to buffer Congress folks who support reform from the hostility they will face from constituents who don't. History may well characterize the current health care reform drama as the "Christmas/Easter Miracle on Pennsylvania Avenue." True reform came to life—died several premature deaths at the hands of its crucifiers—then was resurrected into law during the week before Easter.

The political miracle, however, is only the precursor for what is to follow as Congressional reform-supporters confront the wrath of hostile voters who think the bill is too expensive, unaffordable, unfair to some segments of the health care industry and too generous to others. There is no question many legislators are putting themselves into political harm's way through their votes. I would like to think, however, that those who vote their beliefs and lose their jobs will have the satisfaction of knowing they didn't compromise their beliefs. Conversely, those who voted politically—and not in ways that reflect their beliefs—they will pay the greater price in losing their integrity and satisfying their self-interests. I sympathize with Congress members who challenge themselves with the adage, "If not now, then when?"

What about President Obama? Does the passage of the health care legislation signal his demise as a politician? As a politician, Obama desperately needs to win this debate. He needs Speaker Pelosi to cut the deals—forget about transparency. Make no mistake that this is about to happen.

Obama can still maneuver the votes—at least for now. All the ranting and raving of outraged Republicans cannot stop a health care bill from reaching the President's desk. The only thing the minority party can do at this point is to lick their wounds, cry "foul" and get folks focused on defeating the Democrat's majority in the upcoming mid-term elections. President Obama is well aware such a reality is apt to happen whether the reform bill passes or not. That's politics as usual.

The mid-term elections are—in the Grand Scheme of Things—the least the current administration has to worry about. That's why President Obama is willing to forge ahead with his agenda. He knows he is damned if he does and damned if he doesn't when it comes to health care legislation. So why not do what he thinks is the right thing for the country and move on with the rest of the agenda? What is there to lose?

The real test of the Obama administration's worthiness to move beyond a single-term presidency is not going to rest on the success of a health reform bill—however little or much is actually pared down in the President's final version. If the President doesn't score big on jobs, on addressing deficit, winding down the unpopular wars, and strengthening national security, then universal health care access for unemployed, insecure, war-plagued, and deeply indebted American's will not be viewed as a miracle but something that is exacerbating an economic nightmare and foreshadowing a grim future for America.

Covering 30 million more Americans with basic health care access is not going to change the ugly mood among the American voters towards our government's political process. The process, however, hasn't changed. What has changed is the awareness level of the American people toward how the process works. It isn't broken. It continues to work as it has always worked. At this moment in time, the Democrats dominate. They have the power to make the deals—and they will, rest assured! That's why President Obama will have a health care bill on his desk before the Easter break. That's always been the true miracle of Pennsylvania Avenue—that anything so big and consequential can actually get done.

23

"The Shame of Not-for-Profit Expenses"

The nightly news coverage of the questionable practices of not-for-profit reimbursement is only the tip of the iceberg. It is time to re-evaluate the guidelines for what constitutes a not-for-profit single purpose charity.

I think the issue that happens is that some folks pressure the not-for-profit organizations to "behave like real businesses." Translated, that often means thinking in terms of "margin" and not "mission."

Health care is an excellent example. Executive compensation is based on controlling productivity, increasing revenues, decreasing expenses, and showing a healthy bottom line excess revenue over expenses (EROE)—the jargon for explaining "profit."

When a not-for-profit organization begins measuring its success if form of EROE, that is when executive compensation gets out of hand. The head of Catholic

Healthcare West, my old company, now gets 6 million dollars a year compensation. He also received a forgiveness of a couple of million-dollar loan used to buy him two condos in an exclusive building next to Pac Bell Baseball Park in SF. He knocked out the wall between the two so he could have "liveable space."

Sister Julie operated with the same abandon of concern for expenses. She thought nothing of taking 20 board members to an exclusive resort in Hawaii each year—and taking them to expensive dinners where endless bottles of wine costing 70 dollars were poured. I became cynical. I also realized that Julie always wanted the salary and benefits of her subordinate to be increased—because it drove the price of her salary in the system.

Sadly, too often the expense of not-for-profit become an easy way for unscrupulous leaders to live a high on the hog life style at the expense of taxpayers. I was and am among those who now question if there is any need for not-for-profit status for hospitals. That could come to pass if we have true health care reform. There is indeed abuse.

I say with some shame that when I retired I made a base salary of $250k and a bonus of $250k. Was the position worth that salary—I jokingly and cynically say, it is just as justifiable as a university football coach—and ignores the injustices of the relative compensation of others like faculty who make the educational system operate so there can be a football team.

What is the remedy? It is clear to me. We need to have executive compensation for not-for-profits to be no more that X% of the average salary of the employees, and in no case to exceed Y% of the operating revenues of the organization. I also think that the woman who is now the head of United Way was right on in her interview—her $144k salary is a livable salary. Not-for-profits were not meant to compete with the private sector for leadership—that is not their business mission. The not-for-profit organizations need competent leadership—not wall-street driven business moguls.

I would support a bill to severely limit the salary of executives of not-for-profit organizations. I think that would encourage the competent mission-driven folks to focus on the mission of the not-for-profit and not on how much EROE can be generated to create an extravagant executive salary.

I think the CEO of the Catholic Community Services of Lane County makes about 70k. He is a ex-attorney who elected to do the role because he is mission and not financially driven. (Thought rumor has it he made a bundle before leaving the legal field!)

24

"The Sports Illustrated Jinx: Will It Visit Oregon?

I am not normally a superstitious person. However, certain coincidences always increase my heart-rate—especially the so-called "Sports Illustrated Jinx." I need not to remind superstitious fans of the dozens of superstar athletes pictured over the years on the cover of **Sports Illustrated**, only to have great misfortune befall their athletic careers right after the so-called cover story honor!

Oregon fans are going to have one of their own superstars test the efficacy of this must enduring of the sporting world's superstitions. This week a highly talented Oregon runner is to be featured on the cover of **Sports Illustrated** with the caption "The fastest man in football."

The Oregon sophomore DeAnthony Thomas—known by the moniker "the Black Mamba—an allusion to the fastest and deadliest snake in the world—is the SI Cover Story.

With all due respect to both the journalists at the magazine and the subject of their story, there is no getting around the fact DAT as he is known at Oregon is a true phenomenon who is certainly worthy of the attention.

Just consider these statistics. His total games played in since arriving at Oregon are seventeen. In this his first season plus three games this year he has scored an amazing 25 touchdowns.

DAT has averaged 12.1 yards per rush in his career. What is most astounding, however, is this statistic: He has scored on runs of 91, 64, 62, 59, 51, 39, 35, 33, and 29 yards.

Thomas's receptions are equally impressive. He has scored on receptions of 69, 45,41,41,33, and 29 yards.

Oh, and he has also returned two kick-offs for touchdowns!

Not that I'm superstitious, mind you—I just wish the praise could have been reserved for later in this fledging season of the Pac-12 competition. After all, the mighty USC Trojans expectations for running the table and securing the national championship title in 2012—as well a willing the Heisman Trophy for their talented quarterback—was all but squashed with the upset visited upon the self-confident team by Stanford in their season opener.

This week the talent laden # 3 in the national rankings Oregon faces a highly talented University of Arizona team that is also ranked in the top 25 teams (#22).

I don't want to envision all that could go wrong for DAT and the Ducks! I want to believe that DAT will hold on to the ball and not fumble. I want to believe that he will bring his A-game and demonstrate his incredible speed to the benefit of the Duck's powerful offense.

Most of all, however, I don't want some fluke injury or flub to validate the mythology of the SI jinx!

I realize that every superstar football player is always one play away from being sidelined for the rest of a game, or worse, the rest of the season—and/or most terrible—a career ending injury.

DAT is certainly not exempt from this sobering reality. Every player goes into each game with such a reality hanging over his head. Football is indeed a violent sport that requires stamina and conditioning, heads-up awareness of dangerous situations, and, foremost, a lot of just dumb luck.

It always amazes me that a running back like former Oregon great LaMichael James could carry the ball 25-30 times per game and endure the punishment the running back position visits on durable players. I say the same thing as I watch current sensation running back Barner do the same.

I forget that DAT is only 5'9" tall and weighs at the most 175 pounds. Consider that stature in contrast to the 300 pound linemen and the 225 pound linebackers and corners!

I know DAT is shifty and can turn it on and outrun anyone on the field. But, there is always the misfortune of being in the way of the wrong tackler at the right angle to inflict career altering collisions!

Life is tough enough on the football field each week without having to tempt football fate with the hubris of one's photo displayed on the cover of **Sports Illustrated**.

I suppose I should pit the strength of my own religious faith against such foolish superstitious notions as an SI Cover Jinx. So, with such a thought in mind, I am simply going to say the same prayer I say for all players before each game. I pray that DAT and all of his teammates be kept from harm's way and enjoy performing at their peak during the game.

Go Ducks! Let's pray that we can not only Win The Day, but that we can also dispel the mythology of the Sports Illustrated jinx!

25

"Where Does the Buck Stop?"

The caustic and embittered rhetoric of President Barak Obama after the defeat of the Senate compromise legislation on background checks for gun purchasers raises the question that should be in the forefront of all who try to understand the American political scene: where does the buck stop?"

Conventional wisdom would suggest that the buck stops as Harry Truman admonished, on the desk of the country's President and Chief Executive Officer. Instead of the President saying, *"I've got to find better ways to lead my own party and to help it connect with the opposition party to fashion legislation we all know is the wish of the American people,"* what does he say? *"The American people have got to hold their representative accountable in the upcoming election?"*

I thought the President's remarks in his Rose Garden speech were heartfelt. And, it was appropriate to have the remarks introduced by the impassioned plea of the father of one of the victims of the school shootings that took the lives of 20 innocent people.

What was missing was any personal responsibility for the outcome. He accused the Republican Senators for aligning with the NRA political lobbyists and in the same breath criticized the Republicans for politicizing the issue—yet, in his own political frustration he was himself using the defeat as a political platform to set the stage for the 2014 mid-term elections!

I don't blame the President for feeling the frustration he exhibited in the speech. It was a political defeat in which he'd invested a great deal of his political currency—some say more than he spent even on his landmark Affordable HealthCare Act.

What makes me disappointed was that the President missed an opportunity to own the responsibility for the defeat and pledge that he would work to do a better job in the debates ahead to use his leadership to bring such legislation to fruition.

I think the sad unintended consequences of this political defeat—however temporary—is how it underscores the need for President Obama to examine his own leadership style and to own some of the responsibility for looking at how he can improve his Presidential leadership. It

What makes it so difficult for the President to assume some responsibility?

When does the President take a look at his own leadership and begin to own some of the responsibility for leading a political party that is very much embroiled in the political infighting that leads to inaction on a piece of legislation that the vast majority of the American people support?

I did not vote for President Obama in either of his elections. However, I continue to look for some fragments of hope that he will do the right thing and step up to the leadership expectations the American people have for the Presidency.

I have not done any content analysis of the President's public proclamations and speeches during the course of his Presidency. It would be a useful analysis, however, to survey his remarks and to see how often he has assumed "ownership" when something he wants to happen through the political process fails to pass through Congress.

I think what the speech foreshadowed today was the reality that Congress is in a political grid-lock from which there will be no retreat until we elect a new President who knows how to work with congress.

I felt like Obama was almost pouting and fuming and finger-pointing and not willing to even presume that perhaps his style of leadership is what is at the core of the congressional impasse on even relatively non-controversial issues.

In my opinion the failure of President Obama to assume SOME responsibility for the failure of the compromise gun legislation speaks volumes about the failure of his leadership.

Admit it, President Obama, "The Buck Stops on my Desk!"

26

"Why I Do Not Support the President's Decision In the Prisoner Swap"

Anyone who reads this will ask, what special standing does Roger Hite have that warrants giving him space on the editorial page to opine on the most recent Presidential decision to swap one American prisoner for five prisoners held in by the US and considered dangerous enemies?

My standing in this issue is simple. I am an American who has struggled for the past two elections to find reasons to support President Obama. I did not vote for him in either election. I did, however, want him to succeed and was willing to consider each of his programs and plans for addressing serious economic, social, and political conditions in our country. Once elections are over it is time to get on with the business of running the government. I expected our President to focus on the business of government. I expected Congress to cooperate.

Sadly, neither the current Administration or the Congress met my expectations.

When the Affordable Care Act was being debated I rooted for the President to take his party's control of both houses of congress and to do what was necessary to initiate a single-payer national health program that would in effect create a system for all Americans that would be modeled after what I receive as a recipient of Medicare. It works for me and millions of other Americans who do not see it as "socialized medicine." Sadly, such an option was not selected in an effort to create a program that kept the private sector insurance industry in its middle-man role.

It is not necessary to resurrect many of the initiatives for revitalizing the economy that did not come to fruition under the President's administration. Cash for Clunkers, the Stimulus program for "shovel ready" projects, and the investment in "green" industries didn't pay the dividends envisioned.

I am a realist. I know that the best-laid political plans and dreams come and go with each Presidential administration. I know we have gridlock. I blame both parties, not just President Obama. Certainly the current administration has its hands full of issues like immigration and security of our borders.

It wasn't until I learned of the President's decision to exchange one American prisoner for five terrorists in our captivity that I think I experienced the proverbial "straw that broke the camel's back."

The camel's back, in my metaphorical imagery, is the pride we have in our American government and the pride we have had over the decades of my lifetime [70 years] that we are held in high esteem throughout the rest of the world. I believe our government can still be a model for the rest of the world.

I was saddened to learn the President "went it alone" without Senatorial support in engineering the prisoner swap. I am certain he felt he was doing the right thing—based on his intelligence that the prisoner was in failing health—and his fear that revealing we were engaged in a swap was going to result in the enemy killing their prisoner. What choice does the President have but to bolster his strongest arguments to support his unilateral decision as our Commander-in-Chief.

I don't share the view that he violated the law—at least technically. He had the power to make his decision.

His argument that one returned soldier who served his country deserved to be returned home—regardless of the price and the circumstances is a bold one.

It is sad that the issue is not one we can celebrate with the President—as he did with the soldier's parents in the Rose Garden. It is one that has circumstances yet to be fully explained or understood about how the soldier became a prisoner of war.

In retrospect, one has to wonder why our President—knowing as he must have surely known about the curious circumstances surrounding the soldier captivity—placed a high priority on championing the swap?

Why did not our President do what would have been consistent with his view that we should get the soldier home at all costs—and irrespective of his alleged deserter status—and simply let the military justice system run its course?

That's my beef in this issue. I could have supported our President grimacing and exchange prisoners—and then dealing with the natural consequences of the soldier's judgment in leaving his duty station. It appalls me that once again a spokesperson for the administration put the spin that "the soldier served with honor."

Unfortunately, the decision seemed to be predicated on the political currency it brought to the President at a time when he wanted to put a capstone on the structure of his legacy of someone who was ending the war and moving on.

If the war against terrorism was a war of territorial boundaries, then certainly leaving Afghanistan would have warranted the swap of prisoners. However, the war against terrorism is not about geopolitical boundaries. Exiting Afghanistan does not signal the end of war—these five prisoners are now free to conspire against and kill Americans.

I think the swap is perhaps the most demoralizing thing President Obama could do for those of us in this country who didn't vote for him, but who wanted him to succeed. His recent decision broke our back and it will surely be reflected in upcoming polls. Americans are lamenting.

27

"The Rest of the Story"

Everyone in my generation has "flashbulb" recollections of where they were when President John F. Kennedy was assassinated by Lee Harvey Oswald in Dallas, Texas on November 22, 1963.

Until now, few have heard the story recalled by Phillip Knight-Sheen—now a retired former nurse and owner of a national health care staffing organization. I heard the remarkable story because Phil is a trustee at Rocky Mountain University of Health Professions, a small private university in Provo, Utah where I am board chair.

One evening Phil recounted his story of working at the Parkland Memorial Hospital in Dallas where Kennedy was taken and pronounced dead after the assassination. What was remarkable was not that this friend and board colleague was a part of one of the most significant events of American history, but the strange coincidences that surrounded the events.

Phil had his typically British wry sense of humor and distinct traces of a British-accent as he told his story to a group at dinner after one of our board meetings that gathered trustees from across the nation for an annual meeting.

Mr. Knight-Sheen was born and raised in England but came to the U.S. and began working at the Parkland Memorial Hospital as an aide in the emergency room while pursuing his nursing degree training. Those of us who serve with him on the board are frequently entertained with Knight-Sheen keen critiques of American politics in which he compares and contrasts the British and American cultures, especially the differences between socialism and capitalism.

I don't recall how we got on the topic of the Kennedy assassination, but Phil volunteered that he was familiar with the event because he worked at Parkland Memorial Hospital for several years during the early part of his health care career.

On the eve of the assassination he was working in the emergency room when the mortally wounded Kennedy arrived and surgeons tried in vain to preserve his life—though there was according to Knight-Sheen skepticism on the part of some of the surgical team that any intervention should be undertaken. Phil recalled in vivid details the confusion and the crowded conditions in the emergency room—and how he felt as care-givers and secret service bodies crammed into the cramped space.

After preliminary evaluations, it was decided to take Kennedy to surgery. After the unsuccessful surgical intervention, the body was pronounced dead. It was one of Knight-Sheen's responsibilities to take the president's remains and place them in the coffin that was used to transport him to the mortuary.

It wasn't just the realization that this now elderly man had been a part of American History that grabbed my attention that evening. It was what might be called "the rest of the story" that intrigued me.

According to Mr. Knight-Sheen, Parkland Memorial Hospital had been remodeled a couple of years before the assassination of President Kennedy. The result of the remodeling activity was that the obstetrics unit of the hospital was re-located from the first floor to the second-floor of the hospital. The former first-floor obstetrics area was converted to the state-of-the-art emergency room where Kennedy was treated.

It was quite by coincidence that when Jack Ruby shot and wounded Lee Harvey Oswald, Mr. Oswald was also taken to the same hospital emergency room where he died. It was also remarkable that on January 3, 1967 the assassin of Lee Harvey Oswald, Jack Ruby also died in the same emergency room as Kennedy and Oswald!

What few people know was that decades earlier the new-born infant, Lee Harvey Oswald, entered the world in the very space on the first floor where the new-born nursery was housed. He was born in the same hospital where he eventually died. Most extraordinary, however, was the fact that according to Phil Knight-Sheen, Lee Harvey Oswald died in approximately the same location in the hospital where he first entered the world.

Since I first heard the story I have wanted to verify the fact that the hospital was indeed remodeled in the fashion described by my board colleague. I have no reason to doubt the recollection of Mr. Knight-Sheen.

If all the facts are as relayed from the memory of my colleague it is truly a most remarkable coincidence that is indeed worthy of sharing with all who remember each year on the anniversary of the Kennedy Assassination "where they were and what they were doing" on that fateful day.

What are the odds of the assassin Lee Harvey Oswald dying in the same room in the same hospital where he was born? What are the odds, also, that the assassin of the assassin met his demise in the very same space four years later?

Now that's a little known piece of historical trivia worth sharing with everybody to consider each time they recall their own "flashbulb" recollections of where they were when Kennedy was shot.

28

"Saying It is So, Doesn't Make It So"

My father used to admonish me that *"saying something is so, doesn't make it so!"* Such wisdom seems appropriate to pass on to Dr. Matthew Dennis, the UO history professor emeritus after reading his well-written article. In his August 21st editorial he challenged the **Register-Guard's** earlier opinion advocating not to change the name of Deady Hall.

However, just because professor Dennis does a fine job of expressing his view, saying it is so doesn't make it so!

I respectfully disagree with his thesis by challenging the core of his reasoning.

Dr. Dennis praises his profession of historians for uncovering heretofore little known facts about Deady and Dunn. He asserts that *"being armed with our enhanced historical understanding, the renaming question* [renaming Deady Hall] *now enters the realm of 'public memory.'"*

It sounds nice to declare there is such a reality as "public memory" but in fact it is a construct—something that doesn't exist in reality, but serves to allow one to advance an argument. Of course that is precisely what professor Dennis does when he stipulates a definition that *"Public memory is the collective sense of the past that matters to us all—it's the history that ordinary people carry around with them, the big stories that we share that explains our world, helps ground our collective identity, and offers guidance and shape our aspirations."*

One can certainly disagree with this notion that humanity has a collective memory that struggles to bring a cognitive balance to the dissonance created by historical facts over a span of human history.

Dr. Dennis goes on to argue that *"such 'presentism' is not only unavoidable but essential, because the past itself is too vast to recreate in full and because our world changes and we must adjust to it."*

I should not be surprised to see the effort by some to create the persona of a "public" and attribute to it the human quality of having a "memory." Of course like all constructs, saying it is so, doesn't make it so.

Recall how so many of us were upset when the Supreme Court stipulating a corporation was a "person" and therefore enabling the approval of campaign funding in the Citizens United decision! Saying it is so, doesn't make it so!

I abhor racism, sexism, xenophobia, and prejudices against any religious or cultural group. I acknowledge these things existed in the past—covertly or overtly—and still do today.

"Historical correctness," however, seems to be in conflict with "political correctness" in Professor Dennis' article.

Does the construct of "public memory" allow modern thinkers to have the right to "cast the first stone" back into history and erase something that is not acceptable in modern society? Recall the words of Christ challenging those about to stone the adulteress: "*Ye who are free of sin cast the first stone.*

Those who want to condemn past people honored by having their names put on buildings seem to miss the point. Mr. Deady or Mr. Dunn didn't put their names on the buildings. The naming was a reflection of the attitudes, believes, and values of the times. Removing the names from the buildings does not remove the historical fact that Mr. Deady and Mr. Dunn lived in different times—times that historical facts illustrate were sadly, significantly different from modern times.

I fail to see how removal of the names can be "*a prelude to consequential changes*" any more than altering any other historical fact can change any undesirable features of modern society.

Contrary to the R-G editorial, I don't defend leaving the names on the buildings to "symbolizes" how far we have come. The names are factual statements of the values and attitudes of different times. They should be left in place as historical facts.

Let's suppose the names are removed and the buildings *"proudly bear respectable names"* according to the standards and values that reside in a theoretical so-called "public memory." Do we return to yesteryear and find a more respectable name from that period or find a name today that meets our criteria?

Does such an action do anything to right the wrongs of contemporary society where modern history is being written in the inner-cities and ghettos of this country— where many people could give a "rat's ear" about what a building on the University of Oregon campus is named? Shouldn't attention be focused on fixing the wrongs and injustices of modern times rather than worrying about something that can't be fixed in the past?

Even if "public memory" is an accepted construct, the name of a building on the U of O campus is not part of any big story ordinary people carry around to explains our world. How does eliminating the name *"ground our collective identity?"*

Finally, my solution to the "tempest in a teapot" debate over appropriate naming of buildings on the University of Oregon campus is to simply put a price tag on naming rights. Re-name all buildings for anyone willing to pay the highest price for the honor. All buildings could be renamed every generation—assuring the flow of money to the university to reduce the cost of tuition! Of course, then we could argue over how the money was earned!

NOTES

NOTES